OPPOSING VIEWPOINTS® SERIES

Hunting and Conservation

For Reference

Not to be taken from this room

D0905751

Other Books of Related Interest

Opposing Viewpoints Series

Corporate Farming
Development, Land Use, and Environmental Impact
The Politics of Water Scarcity

At Issue Series

Environmental Racism and Classism
Ethical Pet Ownership
Guns: Conceal and Carry

Current Controversies Series

The Economics of Clean Energy
Environmental Catastrophe
The Industrial Food Complex

> "Congress shall make no law … abridging the freedom of speech, or of the press."

First Amendment to the US Constitution

The basic foundation of our democracy is the First Amendment guarantee of freedom of expression. The Opposing Viewpoints series is dedicated to the concept of this basic freedom and the idea that it is more important to practice it than to enshrine it.

OPPOSING VIEWPOINTS® SERIES

Waubonsee Community College
Libraries
Aurora - Sugar Grove - Plano

Hunting and Conservation

Marcia Amidon Lusted, Book Editor

GREENHAVEN
PUBLISHING

Published in 2021 by Greenhaven Publishing, LLC
353 3rd Avenue, Suite 255, New York, NY 10010

Copyright © 2021 by Greenhaven Publishing, LLC

First Edition

All rights reserved. No part of this book may be reproduced in any form
without permission in writing from the publisher, except by a reviewer.

Articles in Greenhaven Publishing anthologies are often edited for length to meet page
requirements. In addition, original titles of these works are changed to clearly present
the main thesis and to explicitly indicate the author's opinion. Every effort is made to
ensure that Greenhaven Publishing accurately reflects the original intent of the authors.
Every effort has been made to trace the owners of the copyrighted material.

Cover image: MyImages - Micha/Shutterstock.com

Library of Congress Cataloging-in-Publication Data

Names: Lusted, Marcia Amidon, editor.
Title: Hunting and conservation / Marcia Amidon Lusted, book editor.
Description: First edition. | New York : Greenhaven Publishing, 2021. |
  Series: Opposing viewpoints | Audience: Grades 9–12.
Identifiers: LCCN 2020000015 | ISBN 9781534506930 (library binding) | ISBN
  9781534506923 (paperback)
Subjects: LCSH: Hunting—Environmental aspects. | Wildlife conservation. |
  Endangered species—Effect of hunting on. | Hunting—Moral and ethical
  aspects.
Classification: LCC SK33 .H827 2021 | DDC 639/.1—dc23
LC record available at https://lccn.loc.gov/2020000015

Manufactured in the United States of America

Website: http://greenhavenpublishing.com

Contents

The Importance of Opposing Viewpoints   **11**

Introduction   **14**

Chapter 1: Does Hunting Benefit Wildlife Conservation Efforts?

Chapter Preface   **18**

1. Trophy Hunting Can Help Conservation in Africa   **20**
   Jason Roussos

2. Trophy Hunting Only Helps the Ultra-Rich Elite   **27**
   Andreas Wilson-Spath

3. Most Justifications for Hunting Can Be   **32**
   Debunked Easily
   Ashley Capps

4. Hunting Helps Preserve Wildlife   **37**
   Brad Fitzpatrick

5. Sport Hunting Is Cruel and Unnecessary   **43**
   PETA

6. Gun Sales Fund Wildlife Programs   **48**
   Sam Schipani

Periodical and Internet Sources Bibliography   **54**

Chapter 2: Does Hunting Create a Culture of Killing Animals for Sport or Gain?

Chapter Preface   **57**

1. Wildlife Smuggling May Pose a Transnational   **59**
   Security Threat as Well as an Environmental One
   Liana Sun Wyler and Pervaze A. Sheikh

2. Environmental Crime Is Considered Transnational   **69**
   Organized Crime
   United Nations Office on Drugs and Crime

3. Inside the Minds of Trophy Hunters   **80**
   Elle Hunt

4. There Is No Sport in Canned Hunting   **88**
   Oliver Milman

Periodical and Internet Sources Bibliography   **96**

Chapter 3: Does Hunting Increase the Risk of Extinction?

Chapter Preface   **99**

1. Poachers Are Moving Some Animals Toward   **101**
   Extinction
   Jessica Phelan

2. Hunting Helps Control Deer Overpopulation   **107**
   Allen Pursell, Troy Weldy, and Mark White

3. "Fear Effects" Can Manage Populations More   **114**
   Effectively Than Lethal Strategies
   Jennie Miller

4. Human Encroachment Is the Biggest Threat to   **120**
   Animal Endangerment
   Jennifer Bove

5. Non-Native Species Have Potential for Conservation   **125**
   Martin A. Schlaepfer, Dov F. Sax,
   and Julian D. Olden

Periodical and Internet Sources Bibliography   **133**

Chapter 4: Do Hunting Laws Contribute to Food Chain Imbalance?

Chapter Preface   **136**

1. Managing Natural Resources Is Complex   **137**
   Shreya Dasgupta

2. Controlled Hunting Is Environmentally Friendly   **144**
   John Mills

3. Threats to Lions, Leopards, and Wolves Endanger   **149**
   Us All
   Robin McKie

4. Fear of Humans Can Ripple Through Food Webs   **154**
    Liza Gross

Periodical and Internet Sources Bibliography   **162**

For Further Discussion   **164**

Organizations to Contact   **166**

Bibliography of Books   **170**

Index   **172**

The Importance of Opposing Viewpoints

Perhaps every generation experiences a period in time in which the populace seems especially polarized, starkly divided on the important issues of the day and gravitating toward the far ends of the political spectrum and away from a consensus-facilitating middle ground. The world that today's students are growing up in and that they will soon enter into as active and engaged citizens is deeply fragmented in just this way. Issues relating to terrorism, immigration, women's rights, minority rights, race relations, health care, taxation, wealth and poverty, the environment, policing, military intervention, the proper role of government—in some ways, perennial issues that are freshly and uniquely urgent and vital with each new generation—are currently roiling the world.

If we are to foster a knowledgeable, responsible, active, and engaged citizenry among today's youth, we must provide them with the intellectual, interpretive, and critical-thinking tools and experience necessary to make sense of the world around them and of the all-important debates and arguments that inform it. After all, the outcome of these debates will in large measure determine the future course, prospects, and outcomes of the world and its peoples, particularly its youth. If they are to become successful members of society and productive and informed citizens, students need to learn how to evaluate the strengths and weaknesses of someone else's arguments, how to sift fact from opinion and fallacy, and how to test the relative merits and validity of their own opinions against the known facts and the best possible available information. The landmark series Opposing Viewpoints has been providing students with just such critical-thinking skills and exposure to the debates surrounding society's most urgent contemporary issues for many years, and it continues to serve this essential role with undiminished commitment, care, and rigor.

The key to the series's success in achieving its goal of sharpening students' critical-thinking and analytic skills resides in its title—

Opposing Viewpoints. In every intriguing, compelling, and engaging volume of this series, readers are presented with the widest possible spectrum of distinct viewpoints, expert opinions, and informed argumentation and commentary, supplied by some of today's leading academics, thinkers, analysts, politicians, policy makers, economists, activists, change agents, and advocates. Every opinion and argument anthologized here is presented objectively and accorded respect. There is no editorializing in any introductory text or in the arrangement and order of the pieces. No piece is included as a "straw man," an easy ideological target for cheap point-scoring. As wide and inclusive a range of viewpoints as possible is offered, with no privileging of one particular political ideology or cultural perspective over another. It is left to each individual reader to evaluate the relative merits of each argument—as he or she sees it, and with the use of ever-growing critical-thinking skills—and grapple with his or her own assumptions, beliefs, and perspectives to determine how convincing or successful any given argument is and how the reader's own stance on the issue may be modified or altered in response to it.

This process is facilitated and supported by volume, chapter, and selection introductions that provide readers with the essential context they need to begin engaging with the spotlighted issues, with the debates surrounding them, and with their own perhaps shifting or nascent opinions on them. In addition, guided reading and discussion questions encourage readers to determine the authors' point of view and purpose, interrogate and analyze the various arguments and their rhetoric and structure, evaluate the arguments' strengths and weaknesses, test their claims against available facts and evidence, judge the validity of the reasoning, and bring into clearer, sharper focus the reader's own beliefs and conclusions and how they may differ from or align with those in the collection or those of their classmates.

Research has shown that reading comprehension skills improve dramatically when students are provided with compelling, intriguing, and relevant "discussable" texts. The subject matter of these collections could not be more compelling, intriguing, or urgently relevant to today's students and the world they are poised to inherit. The anthologized articles and the reading and discussion questions that are included with them also provide the basis for stimulating, lively, and passionate classroom debates. Students who are compelled to anticipate objections to their own argument and identify the flaws in those of an opponent read more carefully, think more critically, and steep themselves in relevant context, facts, and information more thoroughly. In short, using discussable text of the kind provided by every single volume in the Opposing Viewpoints series encourages close reading, facilitates reading comprehension, fosters research, strengthens critical thinking, and greatly enlivens and energizes classroom discussion and participation. The entire learning process is deepened, extended, and strengthened.

For all of these reasons, Opposing Viewpoints continues to be exactly the right resource at exactly the right time—when we most need to provide readers with the critical-thinking tools and skills that will not only serve them well in school but also in their careers and their daily lives as decision-making family members, community members, and citizens. This series encourages respectful engagement with and analysis of opposing viewpoints and fosters a resulting increase in the strength and rigor of one's own opinions and stances. As such, it helps make readers "future ready," and that readiness will pay rich dividends for the readers themselves, for the citizenry, for our society, and for the world at large.

Introduction

> *"All hunters should be nature-lovers.*
> *It is to be hoped that the days of mere*
> *wasteful, boastful slaughter are past*
> *and that from now on the hunter*
> *will stand foremost in working for*
> *the preservation and perpetuation of*
> *wild life, whether big or little."*
>
> *US President Theodore*
> *Roosevelt*

Throughout human history, hunting animals for meat was often vital to survival. It is estimated that humans have been hunting for more than three million years. Before early humans learned how to grow crops and raise domesticated animals, their existence depended on hunting wild animals for food as well as gathering edible plants. Animals also provided skins that could be used for warm clothing and bones that could be used to make tools and weapons.

As societies developed, hunting often became an activity for the wealthy to pursue as a leisure activity. During the Middle Ages, members of the nobility, who owned land, had the right to hunt, and the poor did not. However, eventually people began buying their food, including meat, and fewer families had to rely on hunting as a way to survive.

Today, most people buy their meat from a grocery store or supermarket, and many of the people who still hunt do so for sport rather than necessity, whether or not they do eat the meat of the animals that they kill.

Hunting has become controversial because there are those who feel that hunting and killing any animal is morally wrong. Their argument is that killing any animal is an act of cruelty that causes extreme pain and suffering. They feel this is especially true in those who hunt for sport or pleasure, rather than out of necessity. It is even argued that most game birds and animals do not provide enough sustenance to make hunting them for food even worthwhile.

There is also a very strong feeling against trophy hunting, which is the practice of shooting animals (especially big game and animals that are exotic, such as tigers, elephants, or bears) and then keeping part or all of the preserved animal as a souvenir. Often it is the strongest and healthiest members of an animal species that are killed for trophies, which means that the species is deprived of the best animals to carry on its bloodline. Those who oppose hunting also feel that it is dangerous, not only to people who are injured or killed in firearms accidents while hunting, but also to animals such as deer, which sometimes collide with vehicles when running from hunters.

Those who support hunting feel that it is more than just a sport. It can also be a method for controlling animal populations such as deer, whose overpopulations threaten the health of the environment. Because of suburban sprawl and the destruction of natural habitats, animals are coming into closer contact with people within their own neighborhoods. Especially with species such as white-tailed deer, whose populations have greatly increased in urban areas, the decline in natural predators like wolves and cougars has allowed these populations to explode. Hunting is a way to keep the deer population in check, as well as reducing the threat of Lyme disease from the ticks that deer carry.

Hunters also argue that hunting is natural, and that at some point in evolutionary history, every animal, including humans, has been either a predator or prey. They also disagree with the idea that hunting is dangerous, claiming that sports such as football, boxing, or even biking are actually more likely to cause injuries to participants.

As an activity, hunting is decreasing, according to a 2016 survey conducted by the US Fish & Wildlife Service. At that time, 11.5 million Americans identified themselves as hunters, a drop of 16 percent from the 2011 survey.[1] However, a 2017 survey of Americans showed that 87 percent of the people surveyed felt it was acceptable to hunt for food, although only 37 percent felt it was acceptable to hunt for trophies.[2] Going forward, it is possible that if a change in the economy leaves some families struggling to buy food, then hunting might once again increase. Regardless, hunting and animal conservation are issues that will continue to create strong feelings among people in the United States.

Opposing Viewpoints: Hunting and Conservation attempts to reconcile the connections between the two concepts. In chapters titled "Does Hunting Benefit Wildlife Conservation Efforts?" "Does Hunting Create a Culture of Killing Animals for Sport or Gain?" "Does Hunting Increase the Risk of Extinction?" and "Do Hunting Laws Contribute to Food Chain Imbalance?" viewpoint authors examine pertinent issues regarding hunting and conservation in today's society from a diverse array of perspectives.

Endnotes

1. 2016 National Survey of Fishing, Hunting, and Wildlife-Associated Recreation." US Fish & Wildlife Service, 2016. https://wsfrprograms.fws.gov/subpages/nationalsurvey/nat_survey2016.pdf.
2. Byrd, Elizabeth et al. "Perceptions of Hunting and Hunters by US Respondents." Animals : an open access journal from MDPI vol. 7,11 83. 4 Nov. 2017. https://www.ncbi.nlm.nih.gov/pmc/articles/PMC5704112

OPPOSING
VIEWPOINTS®
SERIES

CHAPTER 1

Does Hunting Benefit Wildlife Conservation Efforts?

Chapter Preface

One of the biggest controversies surrounding the issue of hunting is whether the practice actually helps with wildlife and environmental conservation, or if that is simply a justification for a sport that many people consider to be inhumane and unnecessary.

For one thing, fees collected from hunting license applications often fund state essential conservation programs to preserve natural habitats. These fees also go toward controlling species that are at risk of becoming overpopulated due to the loss of many predator species.

Opponents of hunting, however, argue that it is hunting itself that is reducing the population of large predators and prey. In the case of trophy hunting, where big game species like lions and elephants are killed for sport and often preserved as trophies of the hunter's skill, hunters claim that the fees for trophy hunting help poor economies in places like Africa. However, hunting opponents point to the risk of extinction of these species, and that most local economies do not actually benefit from the visits of hunters.

Opinions about hunting and conservation also vary widely depending on the region. In some parts of the United States, there is a strong hunting culture, and people often rely on wild game for meat to feed their families, particularly over the winter. In other places hunting is not as common and those who are opposed to it comprise a larger majority.

There can be clashes between those who support conservation and believe that wildlife should be part of that conservation, rather than funding state agencies to do conservation work, and those who believe that everyone has a right to hunt for food or for sport, and that their hunting controls overpopulation that might otherwise affect habitats, both animal and human.

The issue of hunting and conservation, and whether they support each other or are inherently two opposing perspectives, is not one that can be easily resolved. This is especially true when the debate pits animal rights advocates against those who believe that hunting can be beneficial both to human hunters and animal habitats. Which side is the right side? The viewpoints that follow offer information that may persuade you one way or the other.

> "There is absolutely no doubt that the
> future of African wildlife is bleak.
> Habitat loss threatens to destroy
> all forms of biodiversity, while
> unselective and indiscriminate illegal
> poaching adds to it."

Trophy Hunting Can Help Conservation in Africa

Jason Roussos

In the following viewpoint, written as an open letter, Jason Roussos argues that trophy hunting in Africa is an issue of critcal importance but also is one that cannot be resolved simply by banning the hunting of large animals. The author contends that many other factors must be considered when devising a management plan that conserves wildlife and habitats while also controlling them. One such factor is the needs of local farmers. Jason Roussos is a professional hunter and safari operator and president of the African Professional Hunters' Association. Born and raised in Ethiopia, he graduated from Colorado State University with a degree in wildlife biology.

"Open letter from the President of the African Professional Hunters' Association", by Jason Roussos, African Professional Hunters' Association, June 3, 2019. Reprinted by permission.

As you read, consider the following questions:

1. What are some of the problems that affect local farmers because of wildlife, according to the viewpoint?
2. What is the difference between nonconsumptive management and consumptive management of wildlife?
3. How are those who kill animals for sustenance, and those who are trophy hunters, differ in public opinion?

June 3, 2019

OPEN LETTER FROM THE PRESIDENT OF THE AFRICAN PROFESSIONAL HUNTERS' ASSOCIATION

Unless you have been to Africa and ventured beyond the well-travelled roads and comfortable accommodations found in many of the continent's great national parks, you will never understand the real reason why Africa's precious wildlife is in such peril. You will never see firsthand what poor rural Africans must deal with to just survive on a day-to-day basis, often in direct conflict and competition with wildlife. You will never understand the persecution that African wildlife is facing at the hands of illegal poachers. But above all, you will never see how much habitat is being destroyed every day to sustain the booming human population.

There is absolutely no doubt that the future of African wildlife is bleak. Habitat loss threatens to destroy all forms of biodiversity, while unselective and indiscriminate illegal poaching adds to it.

Only a coordinated effort that incorporates a diversity of scientifically sound management practices will reap long- term solutions. There is no one "fix-all" strategy to conserving African wildlife. The only way to achieve success is to implement multiple conservation and management practices that work together for one common goal—the continued survival of wildlife and habitat protection.

HUNTERS AS CONSERVATIONISTS

Hunters are among the most ardent conservationists around.

Theodore Roosevelt, the founder of the National Wildlife Refuge System and a hunter himself, knew it.

"In a civilized and cultivated country, wild animals only continue to exist at all when preserved by sportsmen," the 26th president of the United States said years ago. "The excellent people who protest against all hunting, and consider sportsmen as enemies of wildlife, are ignorant of the fact that in reality the genuine sportsman is by all odds the most important factor in keeping the larger and more valuable wild creatures from total extermination."

Department of the Interior officials know it today.

"Hunters are a driving force behind funding many of our nation's conservation efforts," a 2017 Interior Department blog said. "After the extinction of the passenger pigeon and the near elimination of the bison and many migratory bird species in the early 1900s, Americans realized the impacts humans could have on wildlife. To ensure that there would be animals to hunt in the future, hunters began to support programs that helped maintain species populations and protected habitat for wildlife."

Hunters—along with anglers—also were the driving force behind the North American Model of Wildlife Conservation, a set of wildlife

No matter how distasteful certain practices or techniques may be to some individuals or organizations, if they achieve conservation success then they cannot be shunned. How successful a conservation effort is in an area must be judged not by the survival of individual animals but rather by the species' overall population trend. If over time some animals are killed, but the overall population of a species in that area remains stable or increases, then that conservation practice must be deemed successful.

Conservation must be viewed as a brick wall where each brick represents a different management technique or practice. Hunting, photographic safaris, game breeding, and zoos that educate visitors about wildlife are all examples of the various "bricks" in the management principles established more than a century ago that declare that wildlife belongs to everyone, not just the rich and privileged.

These days, hunters directly support wildlife conservation in many ways.

Through the Duck Stamp, hunters help protect and restore habitat for migratory waterfowl and other birds and wildlife. The stamp, formally called the Federal Migratory Bird Hunting and Conservation Stamp, is required as a license for waterfowl hunting. For every dollar spent on Duck Stamps, ninety-eight cents go directly to purchase vital habitat or acquire conservation easements within the National Wildlife Refuge System.

Through the Federal Aid in Wildlife Restoration Act, more commonly known as the Pittman-Robertson Act, hunters fund a range of conservation programs. The act sends revenue from an excise tax on firearms, ammunition and other related equipment to state wildlife agencies to be used for wildlife conservation projects, hunter education and outdoor recreation access. These annual payments to state fish and wildlife agencies have resulted in the recovery of deer, turkeys and many non-game species—with benefits to hunters and non-hunters alike.

"Hunters as Conservationists," US Fish and Wildlife Service

conservation wall. Anytime a brick is removed, it compromises the overall stability of the wall.

Unless both non-consumptive management (where wildlife is not killed) and consumptive management (where wildlife is killed) are utilized side-by-side, conservation will never reach its full potential. Areas such as national parks are set aside for non-consumptive use and are safeguarded from a national level specifically to protect wildlife and wildlife habitat. As the cornerstone of the conservation wall, African national parks play a critical role in conservation. Nonetheless, national parks only cover a fraction of the landmass where wildlife exists in Africa. In fact, in many African countries it is the areas outside these nationally protected lands that harbor more wildlife—not by density, but by total count. In Tanzania, for example, only 7% of the country's land mass is allocated to National Parks, whereas hunting areas make up 32%, thus harboring a much greater wildlife population.

The countries that have adopted and implemented a multiple-use approach to wildlife management are the ones that have succeeded the best at conserving their wildlife resources. Namibia is a prime example of how a country that utilizes both consumptive and non-consumptive wildlife management has seen its wildlife numbers increase in recent years. Kenya, on the other hand, only utilizes non-consumptive management practices and has seen wildlife numbers outside of protected areas plummet over the same time frame. Globally, the country that currently manages its wildlife resources in the most successful and scientifically-sound manner is the United States of America, where multiple-use is the fundamental driving force behind that success.

Over the last few years, African nations that utilize multiple-use conservation practices, especially in regard to high profile species like lion and elephant, have been specifically targeted because of their use of trophy hunting as a consumptive management tool. Trophy hunting is one of the many types of consumptive management practices that occurs in a multi-use system. Other consumptive management practices include meat hunting, trapping, and culling. People who hunt for subsistence or for meat are not facing the same backlash that trophy hunters are. Trophy hunters are portrayed as killing for "sport" or for "fun," and for people who do not fully understand the critical role it plays, this understandably stirs up very strong emotions against the practice. However, what is most relevant when discussing trophy hunting and its role in conservation should be none other than its final outcome on wildlife populations.

In simple terms, trophy hunting is utilized when it is necessary to have a minimal biological impact on the overall wildlife population, while at the same time maximizing the money generated to conserve that species. The only way to achieve this is to selectively harvest only old males, many of which are far past their reproductive prime, while charging top dollar to do so. Meat hunters, on the other hand, do not pay large amounts of money to shoot an animal and are far less selective than trophy hunters when harvesting an animal. The reality is that meat hunters often harvest females as well as younger animals. This is perfectly acceptable in circumstances where a wildlife population needs to be controlled or reduced. Trophy hunting, however, is utilized when dealing with a wildlife population that managers are trying to increase, hence the need to generate large amounts of money for conservation efforts while at the same time only affecting a specie's overall population by a negligible amount.

With all the recent hype surrounding trophy hunting, the most important conservation consideration to discuss has unfortunately been sidelined by a torrent of emotionally charged rhetoric from both sides. That consideration should be the final outcome that trophy hunting has on a population in an area and what happens to that wildlife population and its habitat when trophy hunting is stopped. In 1993, for example, elephant hunting in Ethiopia was prohibited. The tropical rainforests of the Gurafarda region harbored approximately 3,000 elephants of which between 10 and 15 were harvested a year. Within the 10 years following the ban there was no rainforest left in the area, let alone any elephant, as is the case today. This scenario would, unfortunately, be the outcome for most African hunting areas following a total ban on hunting or trophy importation.

Critical to the whole trophy hunting debate is to discuss what alternative management practice would be implemented to replace the conservation and financial void that would arise if trophy hunting was stopped. Only in very rare circumstances would non-consumptive tourism be able to replace the money spent by trophy hunters since most hunting areas cannot compete with National Parks when it comes to accessibility, infrastructure, and wildlife density. As a result, they are far less attractive for photographic tourists. The reality is that following a hunting or trophy importation ban, most hunting areas would be left abandoned with no form of protection or wildlife and habitat management in place. This is an outcome that nobody, hunters or anti-hunters alike, would want.

I would urge everyone who is involved in the trophy hunting debate to look past their initial emotions stirred up by the fact someone is legally and intentionally killing African wildlife, and instead focus on the critical conservation brick that is filled by this practice. If trophy hunting is stopped throughout Africa, wildlife will still survive in national parks and other highly protected areas. However, in the areas outside of these places it would be ravished. The question should be as simple as: "Is that a good result for conservation or not?"

Finally, I would challenge anyone who does not live in rural Africa and does not have to deal with dangerous wildlife on a day-by-day basis to refrain from making decisions that restrict what Africans can and cannot do with their own wildlife. Imagine if the populous of Great Britain, or any other densely populated developed nation, had to deal with man-eating Nile crocodiles in its rivers, hungry lions around its cattle farms, and elephants that harass and trample people while knocking down trees and ravishing farms throughout the countryside. Now imagine on top of all of this, the government being told by foreign nations that they were not allowed to manage, utilize and fully benefit from their wildlife in the ways they deemed fit, not only for the species but also for their citizens. I guarantee the outlook of how to manage these species in those countries would be changed dramatically.

Wildlife is a renewable resource that needs to be properly managed in our increasingly crowded world. If any conservation practice that is proven to work in certain areas is stopped, then we have all failed at doing our part to protect our planet's wildlife, and another valuable brick has been lost from the conservation wall.

Jason Roussos
President, African Professional Hunters Association

> *"Every year, thousands of tourists visit South African private nature reserves to see wild animals in unspoilt surroundings. But how many of these travellers know that some of the most luxurious safari destinations and self-declared champions of conservation also allow these iconic animals to be killed by trophy hunters for 'sport'?"*

Trophy Hunting Only Helps the Ultra-Rich Elite

Andreas Wilson-Spath

The issue of whether trophy hunting helps conservation in Africa or is increasingly contributing to the permanent loss of big game animals, is a constant debate for the owners of African private nature reserves. In the following viewpoint, Andreas Wilson-Spath touches on some of the controversies over trophy hunting, as well as the need for these groups in addition to national parks to find ways of funding their facilities. Andreas Wilson-Spath is a part-time freelance writer and ex-geologist who lives and works in Cape Town, South Africa.

"Does Trophy Hunting Really Benefit Conservation and Local Communities?" by Andreas Wilson-Spath, Conservation Action Trust, February 5, 2019. Reprinted by permission.

As you read, consider the following questions:

1. What is the difference in missions between nature reserves and the tourist lodges found within them?
2. What are the two most common methods of generating income for nature reserves?
3. What are some of the scandals surrounding trophy hunting in Africa?

Every year, thousands of tourists visit South African private nature reserves to see wild animals in unspoilt surroundings. But how many of these travellers know that some of the most luxurious safari destinations and self-declared champions of conservation also allow these iconic animals to be killed by trophy hunters for "sport"?

Exclusive private nature reserves such as Timbavati, Umbabat, Klaserie and Balule on the western boundary of the Kruger National Park claim that they need the income from trophy hunting to remain viable.

Don Scott, co-owner of the Tanda Tula tented camps in Timbavati, bemoans the fact that as a non-profit organisation they receive no government funding and have to bear the full cost of running the reserve.

In doing so, he neatly sidesteps the fact that while the reserve itself may be run on a not-for-profit basis, the expensive tourist and hunting lodges located within its borders most certainly are not. Why should private land and lodge owners not pay full operational costs to support their profitable enterprises?

Besides, reserves such as Timbavati draw enormous benefits from being physically connected to the vastly larger ecosystem of the adjoining national park. Fences between Timbavati and the Kruger National Park were removed in 1993 and the considerable profits in access, prestige and natural services the private reserve derives from this connection are difficult to estimate in financial terms and greatly outweigh the onus of having to pay for running costs.

Far from not getting subsidies, Timbavati, in effect, continuously receives contributions from a publicly owned entity.

Conservation Levies vs Trophy Hunting

Scott points out that Timbavati "relies on income generated from two forms of sustainable utilisation—photographic tourism and trophy hunting." He appears surprised that by raising the conservation levies charged to Timbavati's photographic tourists, the reserve has recently been able to significantly increase the proportion of revenue generated in this way, compared with trophy hunting.

This is hardly a groundbreaking revelation. Private nature reserves throughout Africa have long managed to run financially sustainable operations without having to rely on income from commercial hunting.

Many of the high-paying visitors to reserves such as Timbavati would undoubtedly be willing to pay conservation levies that would guarantee that no trophy killing happens at their chosen holiday spot. Scott himself notes that Timbavati's conservation levies are less than a third those charged in other parts of Africa.

He writes that "it would be a great achievement for the conservation levies to, one day, fully cover the operational expense budget of the Timbavati." Given that many others have demonstrated that this is possible right now, why can't that "one day" be today?

Perhaps it is time for reserves such as Timbavati to acknowledge trophy hunting for what it is: A hugely profitable indulgence for a super-rich elite obsessed with adding as many exotic stuffed animal heads to their collection, rather than a necessary income stream for landowners.

Limited Conservation Value

So what's on Timbavati's "sustainable utilization" menu for trophy hunters in 2019? A total of 68 animals representing 11 species, including 25 Cape buffalo, two hippo, three giraffe, three spotted hyena and, perhaps most controversially, 10 elephant. Umbabat, Klaserie and Balule provide similar offerings, including 37 additional elephant.

While "environmental sustainability" and "conservation" are themes that are touted repeatedly in the marketing materials of these reserves, their active participation in commercial hunting puts them on the wrong side of a global consensus that has debunked the supposed conservation value of the industry.

Assessing commercial hunting in South Africa, Namibia, Zimbabwe and Tanzania, a 2016 report by the Democratic Party staff of the US House Committee on Natural Resources concludes that "significant questions remain about whether or not trophy hunting is sustainable" even where it is comparatively well managed. Other studies demonstrate the detrimental impact hunting for trophies can have on African wildlife populations.

In South Africa, commercial hunting has been marred by scandals involving the captive breeding of lions for canned hunts and a number of private nature reserves have come under fire for their trophy-hunting practices. In 2017, for instance, Timbavati was criticized for seeking permission to hunt an international-standard trophy tusker elephant, and in 2018, hunters in Umbabat shot dead a well-known pride male lion using bait, despite landowner requests not to kill this much-loved lion.

In 2018 a professional hunter in Balule was convicted for conducting an illegal hunt in the reserve and killing a collared research elephant. Also in Balule later in the year, a hunter took 13 shots to kill a young elephant in sight of horrified tourists.

Such activities are doing irreparable damage to South Africa's conservation credentials and stand to cost the country millions in revenue from outraged tourists looking for an ethical holiday experience in the African bush.

Little Help for Local Communities

Yet another assertion made by the pro-hunting lobby is that revenues earned contribute to the economic development of rural communities in surrounding areas. In reality, such benefits are limited and routinely overstated by pundits.

Instead of taking a proactive approach, reserves such as Timbavati seem to trust in a trickle-down theory of local economic development, suggesting that their mere existence will somehow lift locals out of poverty.

The fallacy of this posture is confirmed by Martina Segage's 2015 Masters dissertation, for which she surveyed 99 households in Timbavati Village, concluding that the adjacent reserve "is yet to contribute towards local economic development because its practice is devoid of community development principles."

Scott writes of "finding innovative ways to help local communities derive income from wildlife activities," but the only planned benefit for the reserve's neighbours he mentions for 2019 is the intention to donate the revenue earned from two commercial buffalo hunts. This, he suggests, will help to forge closer links with the reserve's neighbors.

In a place where some of the planet's poorest people see some of its most wealthy enjoy the beauty of their ancestral homeland, this supposedly generous gesture would be laughable if the situation wasn't quite so tragic.

> *"There are thousands of 'state game farms' across the country artificially breeding animals like deer and pheasants, quail and partridges in the hundreds of thousands and releasing them into hunting ranges."*

Most Justifications for Hunting Can Be Debunked Easily

Ashley Capps

In the following viewpoint, Ashley Capps addresses several arguments made by hunters to support their reasons for hunting. The issues addressed include some of the most common arguments of hunters and non-hunters: the ethics of eating wild animals, whether it is necessary to do so, and if hunting really is necessary for population control. Capps argues these points one by one to argue that hunting can rarely be justified in developed societies. Ashley Capps is a poet, freelance writer and editor, and vegan activist.

As you read, consider the following questions:

1. Do most North American hunters hunt to survive?
2. How many deer farms are in Wisconsin?
3. Why does the author use other sources in her arguments against hunting?

"Hunting for Wildlife Population Control and Ethical Eating?" by Ashley Capps, Free from Harm, January 14, 2015. Reprinted by permission.

Is hunting animals morally superior to buying them in the store? We so often hear from hunters who make the case that while factory farming is wrong, there is nothing unethical about eating animals who have been hunted in the wild. After all, the reasoning goes, the animals live a completely natural life just as nature intended, and die more quickly, and with less fear and pain than they would experience with other predators.

But all of this begs the question of necessity. Most North Americans and Europeans (and many others) who hunt do not do so because they *have to* in order to survive. Most of these hunters shop at grocery stores for at least some portion of their food, stores where they have access to dried beans, nuts, grains, produce and other nutritious plant proteins. In such cases, hunting animals for food is unnecessary, and, like farming animals, constitutes the infliction of violence and death on animals we have no need to harm at all.

As Brian Luke writes in *Brutal: Manhood and the Exploitation of Animals,*

> North American men do not hunt out of necessity; they typically do not hunt to protect people or animals, nor to keep themselves or their families from going hungry. Rather, they pursue hunting for its own sake, as a sport. This point is obscured by the fact that many hunters consume the flesh of their kills with their families, thus giving the appearance that hunting is a subsistence tactic. A close reading of the hunting literature, however, reveals that hunters eat the flesh of their kills as an ex post facto attempt at morally legitimating an activity they pursue for its own sake. The hunter often portrays himself as providing for his family through a successful kill and "harvest." This posture seeks to ritually reestablish a stereotypical masculine provider role less available now than may once have been. In reality hunting today is typically not a source of provision but actually drains family resources. Deer hunters, for example, spend on average twenty dollars per pound of venison, once all the costs of equipment, licenses, transportation, unsuccessful hunts, and so forth are calculated.

Hunting as Population Control or Conservation?

"Hunting is necessary for population control." This is the main defense from the hunting establishment that the public has come to widely believe. This false narrative frames hunting, not as sport or leisure, but as essential conservation work, based on an appeal to fear, warning that wildlife populations will spiral out of control and become a nuisance to communities without their intervention. This may explain why even as the hunting population has been steadily declining in recent years, the other 95% representing the non-hunting public still passively supports hunting, believing it to be a necessary evil.

The reality is that there are thousands of "state game farms" across the country artificially breeding animals like deer and pheasants, quail and partridges in the hundreds of thousands and releasing them into hunting ranges. In Wisconsin alone the state currently registers 372 "deer farms," according to the Wisconsin

Basic Facts About Deer Farms in Wisconsin

The following reflects the deer farm industry in Wisconsin as of June 26, 2018:

Number of registered deer premises in Wisconsin	372
Number of hunting ranches	76 of the 372
Number of premises enrolled in the CWD herd status program	168
Number of farms with a CWD positive test since 2001	23
Number of herds depopulated as a result of a CWD positive	13

Department of Agriculture, Trade and Consumer Protection. And when a disease outbreak occurs on these farms, entire herds are "depopulated."

Also in Wisconsin, DNR officials explained to us that a recent $1.7 million investment in a pheasant hatchery will allow them to supply 75,000 birds a year to game farms across the state. These birds who have been raised in captivity are so tame they will often freeze when approached by hunters or predators and are unprepared for the dangers posed by cars. Game farms typically teach novice hunters to kick these birds to force them into flight and then shoot them as they fly off.

The population control argument is especially common as a justification for hunting deer. But as Doris Lin writes in, *What Will Happen to Animals If Everyone Goes Vegan?*

> Hunters sometimes argue that if they were to stop hunting, the deer population would explode. This is a false argument, because if hunting were to stop, we would also stop the practices that increase the deer population. State wildlife management agencies artificially boost the deer population in order to increase recreational hunting opportunities for hunters. By clearcutting forests, planting deer-preferred plants and requiring tenant farmers to leave a certain amount of their crops unharvested in order to feed the deer, the agencies are creating the edge habitat that is preferred by deer and also feeding the deer. If we stop hunting, we would also stop these tactics that increase the deer population.

And in *Scientific Arguments Against Hunting*, Lin writes,

> Big "game" animals like white-tailed deer and black bears rarely exceed their biological carrying capacity—the maximum number of individuals the ecosystem will support without threatening other species. If they exceed that number, a lack of food will kill the weakest individuals, and will also cause the pregnant females to resorb embryos and have fewer offspring. The strongest will survive and the population will become healthier.

Unlike nature, hunters select the small and the weak to survive—reverse evolution. Instead of targeting the young, old, or sick individuals, hunters kill the largest, strongest males. Because hunters prefer large males with big horns, bighorn sheep in Alberta, Canada are now smaller, with smaller horns, compared to thirty years ago. And because hunters prefer to kill elephants with tusks, the African and Asian elephants that have a genetic mutation that leaves them tuskless are now dominating those populations.

> *"There are hundreds of relevant cases where regulated hunting has helped protect wildlife populations and dozens of outstanding hunter-based conservation organizations … that are on the front lines of wildlife preservation."*

Hunting Helps Preserve Wildlife

Brad Fitzpatrick

In the following viewpoint Brad Fitzpatrick argues that hunting actually does help with the preservation of wildlife and the conservation of habitats. The author provides six specific examples of animal species that have recovered in number due to the fees and contributions of hunters and hunting organizations to the management of these animals and their habitats. Brad Fitzpatrick has written for various outdoor publications, including Petersen's Hunting, Outdoor Life, Gun World, *and* Sports Afield, *and is a contributing editor at* Rifle Shooter.

"6 Examples Where Hunting Helped Preserve Wildlife," by Brad Fitzpatrick, Outdoor Sportsman Group, July 25, 2016. Reprinted by permission.

As you read, consider the following questions:

1. What might be some of the reasons why wildlife and hunting organizations work toward preserving species and habitats?
2. What are some of the methods used to generate income from hunters?
3. Do you think the author provides enough evidence that "hunters do more than their share when it comes to the preservation of wildlife and wild places"?

In recent years regulated hunting has become a scapegoat for so-called conservation organizations.

These groups often claim that hunting is not an effective means of preservation and seek to paint sport hunters as villains when wildlife populations decline.

And while it is true that wildlife faces increased threats around the world—primarily a result of habitat loss in the wake of burgeoning human populations, unsustainable agricultural, mining practices and a growing black market for the trade of animal parts—regulated hunting has proven to be an effective means of protecting wildlife and, most importantly, the habitat they require to survive.

Statistics don't lie, though, and there is plenty of evidence that hunters do more than their share when it comes to the preservation of wildlife and wild places.

Statistics Don't Lie

According to the National Shooting Sports Foundation, America's twelve million hunters pump almost $25 billion dollars into the US economy annually, more than a billion dollars of which goes towards licenses, tags, and fees for conservation.

Conservation groups funded by hunter dollars have preserved millions of acres of vital habitat in North America. But the positive economic impact of hunting isn't limited to this continent; the market research, statistics and economic firm Southwick Associates found that hunters inject more than $426 million into the African economy each year and support 53 million jobs on that continent.

There are hundreds of relevant cases where regulated hunting has helped protect wildlife populations and dozens of outstanding hunter-based conservation organizations like Ducks Unlimited, SCI Foundation and the Rocky Mountain Elk Foundation that are on the front lines of wildlife preservation, but here's a look at six instances where hunters and the funds they help generate have preserved habitat and protected wildlife.

Some, like the case of the whitetail deer, will be familiar to many hunters. Others, like the current situation with Bukharan markhor in Tajikistan, are relatively unknown to many and underreported by the world press. So, the next time that someone claims that hunters are bad for wildlife preservation you can present them with the facts, and the facts show that regulated hunting and funds generated by sportsmen and women help protect game.

Waterfowl

The first settlers to Canada's wide-open central prairies stated that there were so many ducks and geese that the birds "blacked out the sun," but in the decades that followed things changed.

By the 1930's much of the prairie pothole region of Canada had been drained for agriculture. America's greatest waterfowl breeding habitat was shrinking and so were waterfowl numbers.

A group of hunters combined their efforts and finances and started an organization that became known as Ducks Unlimited, and with money generated by waterfowl hunters the group began funding aerial surveys, preserving marshlands and raising international awareness about the need to protect waterfowl habitat.

Dozens of species of ducks and geese have benefitted from these efforts—and so have generations of hunters and outdoor enthusiasts. To date Ducks Unlimited has managed to preserve more than twelve million acres of valuable waterfowl habitat in North America, proving that hunter-based conservation works.

Bukharan Markhor

Never heard of the Bukharan Markhor? You're not alone. This rare mountain Caprid (goat) lives in the remote and rugged mountains of Tajikistan. In the early 2000's residents of poor mountain villages were afraid these wild goats, with their magnificent shaggy coats and spiral horns, would eventually be killed out by poachers.

Word reached conservation organizations including IUCN (International Union for Conservation of Nature), Conservation Force, CIC (International Council for Game and Wildlife Conservation) and Panthera, and funds were made available to conduct camera trap surveys, monitor populations and fight poaching operations in the area.

As a result, markhor numbers increased dramatically (a two to three-fold increase in just five years) and in 2013 it was determined that six hunting permits would be issued.

The funds generated from these hunts provided significant capital for poor rural communities and money to help fight poaching rings. Most importantly, the funds have helped show local people that sustainable hunter-based conservation works.

Cape Buffalo

Africa's cape buffalo has a reputation for truculence, but these wild bovids represented a very different kind of threat to farmers. Buffalo carry diseases that can effect domestic cattle—most notably rinderpest, which is fatal to livestock.

As a result buffalo were extirpated across wide ranges of the African continent to make way for cattle. In addition, buffalo were slaughtered commercially for meat or killed in the midst of bloody wars in Mozambique, Zimbabwe, and Angola. But the funds generated by hunters have made buffalo a very valuable species, and these animals are far better adapted to the fragile African landscape than domestic stock.

In Mozambique's Coutada 11 hunting area alone buffalo numbers have increased from 1,200 in 1994 to more than 20,000 animals today thanks to anti-poaching efforts funded by hunter dollars, solid proof that hunting is a valuable tool for protecting African wildlife.

Whitetail Deer

The whitetail deer is the most widespread, most popular and most valuable big game animal in North America. When the first Europeans landed in North America it is estimated that there were around thirty million whitetail deer, a number that dropped to between three hundred and four hundred thousand by 1900 in the wake of unregulated market hunting.

The precipitous decline of the whitetail deer was accompanied by a nationwide call to preserve our wild resources in the face of industrialization. Theodore Roosevelt helped start the Boone & Crockett Club and hunters began crying out that the preservation of natural resources we would require a balance between consumption and conservation.

After seasons and bag limits were enacted whitetail numbers rebounded sharply to an estimated fifteen million animals today and this species help generate a large portion of the over one billion dollars that hunters invest into our nation's economy every year.

Wild Turkey

Like the whitetail deer, wild turkeys were abundant and widespread when the first Europeans came to this country, but habitat loss and unregulated hunting spurred a decline in turkey populations.

In the 1970's hunters formed the National Wild Turkey Federation which raised funds to preserve and restore valuable turkey habitat and to help reintroduce birds into areas where they had been extirpated.

When NWTF began there were an estimated one-and-a-half million turkeys in the United States, and thanks to the conservation efforts and the funds generated today there are more than seven million birds. NWTF also provides education for young hunters through their Jakes program and the increase in turkey populations has made these birds a valuable game species.

Bighorn Sheep

In the 1800's wild bighorn sheep were common from Mexico to northern Canada, but by the 1960's those populations had declined dramatically. There were multiple causes for this decrease including unregulated hunting in the late nineteenth and early twentieth centuries as well as die-offs that were the result of wild sheep populations contracting diseases from domestic animals that shared the same habitat.

In 1974 a group of sheep hunters decided that if sheep populations were to rebound it was critical that conservation efforts must be put in place immediately. That group of hunters established the Foundation for North American Wild Sheep and funding was provided to monitor and protect remaining bighorn populations.

Today, their efforts along with those of state and provincial wildlife agencies have helped sheep populations to increase three-fold. Other hunter-based organizations have also stepped up to help protect sheep as well; in 2014 SCI partnered with the Arizona Game and Fish Department to reintroduce sheep back to the Santa Catalina Mountains near Tucson.

> "Although it was a crucial part of
> humans' survival 100,000 years ago,
> hunting is now nothing more than
> a violent form of recreation that the
> vast majority of hunters do not need
> for subsistence."

Sport Hunting Is Cruel and Unnecessary

People for the Ethical Treatment of Animals

*In the following viewpoint People for the Ethical Treatment
of Animals (PETA) argues against sport hunting for the
simple reason that it is cruel to animals. The authors use
real-life examples and statistics to make their case and offer
ways that people opposed to hunting can fight it. PETA
is the largest animal rights organization in the world,
working through public education, research, animal rescue,
legislation, special events, celebrity involvement, and
protest campaigns to advocate for animal rights.*

As you read, consider the following questions:

1. What might be the purpose of using grim statistics about
   animals' pain and suffering in this viewpoint?
2. What is meant by saying "nature takes care of its own"?
3. Why do you think the article uses the term
   "canned cruelty"?

"Why Sport Hunting Is Cruel and Unnecessary," People for the Ethical Treatment of
Animals. Reprinted by permission.

Although it was a crucial part of humans' survival 100,000 years ago, hunting is now nothing more than a violent form of recreation that the vast majority of hunters do not need for subsistence.[1] Hunting has contributed to the extinction of animal species all over the world, including the Tasmanian tiger and the great auk.[2,3]

Less than 5 percent of the US population (13.7 million people) hunts, yet hunting is permitted in many wildlife refuges, national forests, and state parks and on other public lands.[4] Almost 40 percent of hunters slaughter and maim millions of animals on public land every year, and by some estimates, poachers kill just as many animals illegally.[5,6]

Pain and Suffering

Many animals endure prolonged, painful deaths when they are injured but not killed by hunters. A study of 80 radio-collared white-tailed deer found that of the 22 deer who had been shot with "traditional archery equipment," 11 were wounded but not recovered by hunters.[7] Twenty percent of foxes who have been wounded by hunters are shot again. Just 10 percent manage to escape, but "starvation is a likely fate" for them, according to one veterinarian.[8] A South Dakota Department of Game, Fish and Parks biologist estimates that more than 3 million wounded ducks go "unretrieved" every year.[9] A British study of deer hunting found that 11 percent of deer who'd been killed by hunters died only after being shot two or more times and that some wounded deer suffered for more than 15 minutes before dying.[10]

Hunting disrupts migration and hibernation patterns and destroys families. For animals such as wolves, who mate for life and live in close-knit family units, hunting can devastate entire communities. The stress that hunted animals suffer—caused by fear and the inescapable loud noises and other commotion that hunters create—also severely compromises their normal eating habits, making it hard for them to store the fat and energy that they need in order to survive the winter.

Nature Takes Care of Its Own

The delicate balance of ecosystems ensures their survival—if they are left unaltered. Natural predators help maintain this balance by killing only the sickest and weakest individuals. Hunters, however, kill any animal whose head they would like to hang over the fireplace—including large, healthy animals who are needed to keep the population strong. Elephant poaching is believed to have increased the number of tuskless animals in Africa, and in Canada, hunting has caused bighorn sheep's horn size to fall by 25 percent in the last 40 years. Nature magazine reports that "the effect on the populations' genetics is probably deeper."[11]

Even when unusual natural occurrences cause overpopulation, natural processes work to stabilize the group. Starvation and disease can be tragic, but they are nature's ways of ensuring that healthy, strong animals survive and maintain the strength of the rest of their herd or group. Shooting an animal because he or she might starve or get sick is arbitrary and destructive.

Another problem with hunting involves the introduction of exotic "game" animals who, if they're able to escape and thrive, pose a threat to native wildlife and established ecosystems.

Canned Cruelty

Most hunting occurs on private land, where laws that protect wildlife are often inapplicable or difficult to enforce. On private lands that are set up as for-profit hunting reserves or game ranches, hunters can pay to kill native and exotic species in "canned hunts." These animals may be native to the area, raised elsewhere and brought in, or purchased from individuals who are trafficking in unwanted or surplus animals from zoos and circuses. The animals are hunted and killed for the sole purpose of providing hunters with a "trophy."

Canned hunts are big business—there are an estimated 1,000 game preserves in the US, with some 5,000 so-called "exotic ranchers" in North America.[12,13] Ted Turner, the country's largest private landowner, allows hunters to pay thousands of dollars to kill bison, deer, African antelopes, and turkeys on his 2 million acres.[14]

Animals on canned-hunting ranches are often accustomed to humans and are usually unable to escape from the enclosures that they are confined to, which range in size from just a few yards to thousands of acres. Most of these ranches operate on a "no-kill, no-pay" policy, so it is in owners' best interests to ensure that clients get what they came for. Owners do this by offering guides who are familiar with animals' locations and habits, permitting the use of dogs, and supplying "feeding stations" that lure unsuspecting animals to food while hunters lie in wait.

While many states have limited or banned canned hunts, there are no federal laws regulating the practice at this time.[15]

Other Victims

Hunting accidents destroy property and injure or kill horses, cows, dogs, cats, hikers, and other hunters. In 2006, then–Vice President Dick Cheney famously shot a friend while hunting quail on a canned hunting preserve.[16] According to the National Shooting Sports Foundation, thousands of injuries are attributed to hunting in the US every year—and that number only includes incidents involving humans.[17]

The bears, cougars, deer, foxes, and other animals who are chased, trapped, and even killed by dogs during (sometimes illegal) hunts aren't the only ones to suffer from this variant of the "sport." Dogs used for hunting are often kept chained or penned and are denied routine veterinary care such as vaccines and heartworm medication. Some are lost during hunts and never found, whereas others are turned loose at the end of hunting season to fend for themselves and die of starvation or get struck by vehicles.

What You Can Do

Before you support a "wildlife" or "conservation" group, ask about its position on hunting. Groups such as the National Wildlife Federation, the National Audubon Society, the Sierra Club, the

Izaak Walton League, the Wilderness Society, and the World Wildlife Fund are pro–sport-hunting, or at the very least, they do not oppose it.

To combat hunting in your area, post "no hunting" signs on your land, join or form an anti-hunting organization, protest organized hunts, and spread deer repellent or human hair (from barber shops) near hunting areas. Call 1-800-628-7275 to report poachers in national parks to the National Parks and Conservation Association. Educate others about hunting. Encourage your legislators to enact or enforce wildlife-protection laws, and insist that nonhunters be equally represented on the staffs of wildlife agencies.

References

1. National Research Council, "Science and the Endangered Species Act" (Washington, D.C.: National Academy Press, 1995) 21.
2. Grant Holloway, "Cloning to Revive Extinct Species," CNN.com, 28 May 2002.
3. Canadian Museum of Nature, "Great Auk," 2008.
4. US Fish and Wildlife Service, "2011 National Survey of Fishing, Hunting, and Wildlife-Associated Recreation" (Washington, D.C.: GPO, 2012) 22.
5. US Fish and Wildlife Service 28.
6. Illinois Department of Natural Resources, "How the Program Works," accessed 25 July 2013.
7. Stephen S. Ditchkoff et al., "Wounding Rates of White-Tailed Deer With Traditional Archery Equipment," Proceedings of the Annual Conference of the Southeastern Association of Fish and Wildlife Agencies (1998).
8. D.J. Renny, "Merits and Demerits of Different Methods of Culling British Wild Mammals: A Veterinary Surgeon's Perspective," Proceedings of a Symposium on the Welfare of British Wild Mammals (London: 2002).
9. Spencer Vaa, "Reducing Wounding Losses," South Dakota Department of Game, Fish, and Parks, accessed 25 July 2013.
10. E.L. Bradshaw and P. Bateson, "Welfare Implications of Culling Red Deer (Cervus Elaphus)," Animal Welfare 9 (2000): 3–24.
11. John Whitfield, "Sheep Horns Downsized by Hunters' Taste for Trophies," Nature 426 (2003): 595.
12. Morgan Loew, "Arizona Organization Protects 'Canned' Hunting," CBS5 9 Nov. 2012.
13. CBS News, "Can Hunting Endangered Animals Save the Species?" 60 Minutes 29 Jan. 2012.
14. Robert M. Poole, "Hunters: For Love of the Land," National Geographic Magazine Nov. 2007.
15. Morgan Loew, "Arizona Organization Protects 'Canned' Hunting," CBS5 9 Nov. 2012.
16. Dana Bash, "Cheney Accidentally Shoots Fellow Hunter," CNN.com, 12 Feb. 2006.
17. National Shooting Sports Foundation, "Firearms-Related Injury Statistics," Industry Intelligence Reports 2012.

> *"The lion's share of funding for state wildlife conservation programs comes from the sale of guns, ammunition, and other hunting supplies."*

Gun Sales Fund Wildlife Programs

Sam Schipani

Gun control is a high-priority issue among many Americans, especially in the wake of an increasing occurrence of school shootings, and so it also affects opinions on hunting and its use of firearms. In the following viewpoint, Sam Schipani makes an argument for how the fees generated by guns, ammunition, and licenses plays an important role in wildlife conservation because of the Pittman-Robertson Act of 1937. Sam Schipani was a 2018 Sierra Editorial Fellow. She also has written for Smithsonian, Earth Island Journal, *and* American Farm Publications.

As you read, consider the following questions:

1. Why does the author begin the article with a reference to a school shooting, when she is advocating for hunting?
2. Why is the Pittman-Robertson Act so important to conservation?
3. What are some of the controversial aspects of the Pittman-Robertson Act?

"Did You Know that Gun Sales Fund State Wildlife Programs?" by Sam Schipani, Sierra Club, April 12, 2018. Reprinted by permission.

In the weeks since the horrific Valentine's Day massacre at Marjory Stoneman Douglas High in Parkland, Florida, conversations about gun control have dominated much of the national discourse. All eyes are locked on firearms—who's buying them and how, and what is the degree to which the gun industry's dollars play a role in our political system? But here's something you might have missed: Four days before the March for Our Lives, the federal government distributed $1.1 billion in tax dollars extracted from gun sales to state agencies. The money was earmarked for a specific purpose: wildlife conservation.

This may be surprising, but it isn't new. The lion's share of funding for state wildlife conservation programs comes from the sale of guns, ammunition, and other hunting supplies, thanks to an 80-year-old piece of legislation called the Federal Aid in Wildlife Restoration Act, also known as the Pittman-Robertson Act.

The Pittman-Robertson Act puts an 11 percent tax on sales of firearms, firearm ammunition, archery equipment, and arrow components and distributes it to state governments for wildlife projects. When President Franklin Roosevelt signed the act into law in 1937, it redirected an existing tax on firearms and ammunition to the Department of the Interior to fund state programs for habitat management, wildlife surveys, species reintroduction, and hunter education. The "user-play, user-pay" approach to conservation was revolutionary at the time and provided the foundation for what is known as the North American Model of Wildlife Conservation.

"People often say that this funding model for conservation in America is the greatest story never told," says Ron Regan, executive director of the Association of Fish and Wildlife Agencies. "A lot of people think that fish and wildlife work is funded by taxpayers, when in reality the majority of conservation is funded by sportsmen and -women."

The rules for distributing and spending Pittman-Robertson funds are carefully written. The Department of the Interior distributes the funds according to a set formula among hunter-education programs, projects that require cooperation across multiple states, and state projects. Each state's allocation of funds is based on geographic size and the number of licensed hunters in the state for that year. Prior to receiving funds, states must submit to the interior secretary plans detailing how they will spend the money. Once a plan has been approved, the state must be prepared to pay the full cost up front. The states are later reimbursed for up to 75 percent of that cost through the fund; the remaining 25 percent is usually paid through hunting-license sales. To access the funds, states must also guarantee that hunting-license fees will only be used by their fish and game departments. If the money does not get spent after two years, it is re-allocated to the Migratory Bird Conservation Fund.

The Pittman-Robertson Act has been amended several times over the last 80 years—once in the 1970s to add taxes on handguns and archery equipment for hunter-safety classes and shooting ranges and again in 2000 to further streamline management of the funds. But overall, its ethos has remained the same. Just over a decade after its implementation, a similar act was written for sportfishing: the Federal Aid in Sport Fish Restoration Act, otherwise known as the Dingell-Johnson Act.

State wildlife agencies and the country's wildlife-conservation system are heavily dependent on the funds. According to Regan, the combination of Pittman-Robertson, Dingell-Johnson, and state licensing dollars comprise 70 to 75 percent of the average state fish and wildlife agency budget. In March, the Interior Department distributed $1.1 billion in annual national funding for state wildlife agencies from Pittman-Robertson and Dingell-Johnson funds. Over $12 billion has been collected since 1939 for wildlife conservation thanks to the Pittman-Robertson Act alone.

The legislation has yielded significant results for wildlife conservation. Prior to the development of the act, the populations of hunted species like white-tailed deer, wild turkeys, and wood ducks were at an all-time low. The habitat acquisition and improvement made possible by Pittman-Robertson funds bolstered those species and also helped expand the ranges for American black bears, elk, and cougars. Though Pittman-Robertson funds are limited to programs focused on restoring birds and mammals, nongame species benefit from the conservation programs, too. For example, projects in New York to protect grouse, turkey, and deer habitat were also essential to restoring habitat for the endangered Karner blue butterfly.

"Not only has it helped conserve species that were on the brink of extinction, but more broadly the public at large benefits from these Pittman-Robertson dollars," says Bill Brassard, senior director of communications for the National Shooting Sports Foundation. "It's not just hunters. It's hikers, birdwatchers, and anyone who enjoys these great outdoor spaces and appreciates wildlife. People should know that the funds pay for science that makes decisions about wildlife management."

Some environmental groups, however, are critical of the arrangement. New research shows that hunting-management plans are not always based on sound science, and some animal rights activists argue that the Pittman-Robertson Act skews wildlife-conservation priorities. "The primary problem with the Pittman-Robertson Act is that it is part of a program of wildlife management that prioritizes hunting over meaningful conservation," Marilyn Kroplick, president of In Defense of Animals, wrote in an email to Sierra. "Linking the funding of conservation directly to hunting ensures that game species and their habitats will receive the majority of aid, with populations of these species at times being kept higher than is ecologically healthy."

Meanwhile, there is an overriding sentiment among hunters that since they pay the tax, they should reap the rewards, especially in light of dwindling access to lands for hunting due to private development and urban sprawl. "If hunters are paying for the system, why shouldn't they benefit?" says Whit Fosburgh, president and CEO of the Theodore Roosevelt Conservation Partnership.

"We're losing places to hunt. Hunters are paying into state conservation, so they should be taken care of."

Though the Trump administration is notoriously gun-friendly and Interior Secretary Ryan Zinke has made hunting access a priority, gun sales have slowed during the last year in what the industry is calling the "Trump slump." That's because consumer demand for firearms is tied to whether gun owners believe the government may regulate or remove their weapons. During the Obama administration, for example, gun sales skyrocketed and produced billions more dollars for conservation programs.

But it's not just gun sales that are on the decline: Interest in hunting has seen a precipitous drop-off as well. A US Fish and Wildlife Service survey shows that today, only about 5 percent of Americans hunt—half of what it was 50 years ago—and the decline is expected to accelerate over the next decade. The downturn is likely to have a significant impact on conservation given that state governments rely on the revenue from new hunting licenses to make the 25 percent funding match required by Pittman-Robertson.

"It could have a really catastrophic impact if the numbers continue to go down," says Land Tawney, president and CEO of Backcountry Hunters and Anglers. "Hunters have for a long time been the majority of our management and conservation of wild species. There's a proud history there, but it's also an opportunity now for others to step up and join hunters in carrying on the conservation legacy."

States have some options to fill the gap if hunting numbers continue to decline. Some hunters argue that other outdoor-recreation retailers should also have to pay to play on public lands, especially given that the industry is steadily growing. "With the amount of pressures on our natural resources, whether that's by oil and gas development or urban sprawl or federal policies, it's time for people to step up," Tawney adds. "Even if numbers weren't declining, we still need to expand the pie."

Even as outdoor enthusiasts have been asking themselves whether their outdoor equipment supports the NRA, environmentalists might want to begin examining some of the virtuous connections between wildlife conservation programs and gun sales. Environmentalists and hunters may have common ground in bringing more nuance to the national conversation about guns.

Periodical and Internet Sources Bibliography

The following articles have been selected to supplement the diverse views presented in this chapter.

Terry Anderson, "How Hunting Saves Animals." Hoover Institution, October 29, 2015. https://www.hoover.org/research/how -hunting-saves-animals

Big Game Hunting Adventures, "Is Hunting Conservation? Yes, and Here's Why." https://biggamehuntingadventures.com/heres-how -hunting-promotes-wildlife-conservation

Conservation Hunting, "Conservation." https://www .conservationhunting.com/conservation

Adam Cruise, "Is Trophy Hunting Helping Save African Elephants?" *National Geographic*, November 17, 2015. https://www .nationalgeographic.com/news/2015/11/151715-conservation -trophy-hunting-elephants-tusks-poaching-zimbabwe-namibia

Lincoln Larson, "As Hunting Declines, Efforts Grow to Broaden the Funding Base for Wildlife Conservation." The Conversation, December 15, 2018. https://theconversation.com/as-hunting -declines-efforts-grow-to-broaden-the-funding-base-for-wildlife -conservation-105792

Don Melvin, "Conservation Hunting: Boon to Wildlife or Unjustifiable Sport?" CNN, July 29, 2015. https://www.cnn .com/2015/05/20/us/conservation-hunting-right-or-wrong /index.html

Victor K. Muposhi, Edson Gandiwa, Paul Bartels, and Stanley M. Makuza, "Trophy Hunting, Conservation, and Rural Development in Zimbabwe: Issues, Options, and Implications." *International Journal of Biodiversity*, August 3, 2016. https://www .hindawi.com/journals/ijbd/2016/8763980

Rob Nelson, "Can Hunting Be Conservation?" Untamed Science. https://untamedscience.com/blog/hunting-and-conservation

Rocky Mountain Elk Foundation, "25 Reasons Why Hunting Is Conservation." http://www.rmef.org/Conservation /HuntingIsConservation/25ReasonsWhyHuntingIsConservation .aspx

Nathan Rott, "Decline in Hunters Threatens How US Pays for Conservation." NPR, March 20, 2018. https://www.npr .org/2018/03/20/593001800/decline-in-hunters-threatens-how-u -s-pays-for-conservation

Scientific American, "Does Hunting Help or Hurt the Environment?" November 10, 2009. https://www.scientificamerican.com/article /earth-talks-hunting

Jordan Sillars, "Killing Animals to Save Them? Hunting as Conservation." National Review, November 23, 2019. https:// www.nationalreview.com/2019/11/hunting-as-conservation -sportsmen-incentives-to-protect-endangered-species-habitats

Fran Silverman, "On the Trail: Killing the Myth of Hunting as Conservation." Friends of Animals. https://www .friendsofanimals.org/news/on-the-trail-killing-the-myth-of -hunting-as-conservation

J. Townsend, "Hunting vs Buying Meat: The Traditional Hunter in the Modern World." Harvesting Nature, July 2, 2012. https:// harvestingnature.com/2012/07/02/the-traditional-hunter-in-the -modern-world

CHAPTER 2

Does Hunting Create a Culture of Killing Animals for Sport or Gain?

Chapter Preface

O ne of the most controversial aspects of hunting centers around the idea that, if humans no longer need to hunt in order to survive, then why do they continue to do so? The answer given by many hunters is that they enjoy the sport of hunting, a sport that goes back thousands of years. Cultures such as the Abyssinians, who flourished around 600 BCE, wrote of spectacles where kings killed dangerous animals such as elephants, ibex, ostriches, wild bulls and lions.

During medieval times, kings and nobles frequently engaged in hunting as a leisure sport activity. Linda Kalof, a professor at Michigan State University, wrote, "Ancient … hunts were spectacular displays of royal power and dominance, and always took place with the king's public watching from the sidelines. A successful hunt requires the death of unrestrained wild animals— animals who are hostile, shun or attack humans, and are not submissive to human authority."[1]

Closer to our own time, in the early 1900s, President Theodore Roosevelt frequently hunted big game animals and was photographed with his kills. African safari hunting, which was usually only available to wealthy white men, also became a symbol of the colonial domination of Africa and its people. Anthropologists have hypothesized that by hunting challenging or dangerous animals, even for sustenance, men were sending signals to potential mates and rivals that they were fit and able to take that kind of dangerous risk. Hunting became much more than simply killing wild game for sustenance. It became a culture of killing animals for sport, one that many people argue has allowed harmful activities like poaching, animal cruelty, and illegal hunting to flourish.

However, for many hunters hunting is a lifestyle as well as a sport and, often, a connection to a family tradition. It is an activity that creates camaraderie and fellowship among those who have a tradition of hunting together. In addition to the arguments that hunting has an economic benefit by funding conservation and helps manage wildlife populations, it is also seen as an organic and more humane way to kill animals for food, as opposed to commercial farms and slaughtering methods. Those who trophy hunt large and exotic game animals are not considered to be part of a more honest hunting culture.

Most hunters consider themselves to be stewards of animals and nature, not overenthusiastic killers. But as with any sport or activity, there will be people who operate in ways that are distasteful to this hunting culture, either for profit or for other motives.

Endnotes

1. Weisberger, Mindy. "Hunting Big Game: Why People Kill Animals for Fun." Live Science, May 24, 2017. https://www.livescience.com/59229-why-hunt-for-sport.html

> "*Some terrorist groups may be engaged in wildlife crimes, particularly poaching, for monetary gain. Some observers claim that the participation of such actors in wildlife trafficking can therefore threaten the stability of countries, foster corruption, and encourage violence to protect the trade.*"

Wildlife Smuggling May Pose a Transnational Security Threat as Well as an Environmental One

Liana Sun Wyler and Pervaze A. Sheikh

Despite widespread efforts to protect wildlife, especially endangered species that might be hunted for trophies or profit, there is an illegal international trade in wildlife that sidesteps these protection efforts. As a result, illegal wildlife trafficking continues to rise to new levels, encouraged by lax enforcement of wildlife laws and increasing markets for exotic animals and their parts. In the following excerpted viewpoint, Liana Sun Wyler and Pervaze A. Sheikh provide specific examples of animal species that are at risk because of this illegal trade. Liana Sun Wyler is an analyst in international crime and narcotics at the Congressional Research Service. Pervaze A. Sheikh is a specialist in natural resources policy at the Congressional Research Service.

"International Illegal Trade in Wildlife: Threats and US Policy," by Liana Sun Wyler and Pervaze A. Sheikh, Congressional Research Service, July 23, 2013.

As you read, consider the following questions:

1. Why is illegal trafficking in wild animals such an increasing problem?
2. What methods are traffickers using to illegally poach animals and evade being caught?
3. Why are elephants and rhinos so valuable on the international market?

Global trade in illegal wildlife is a potentially vast illicit economy, estimated to be worth billions of dollars each year. Some of the most lucrative illicit wildlife commodities include elephant ivory, rhino horn, sturgeon caviar, and so-called "bushmeat." Wildlife smuggling may pose a transnational security threat as well as an environmental one. Numerous sources indicate that some organized criminal syndicates, insurgent groups, and foreign military units may be involved in various aspects of international wildlife trafficking. Limited anecdotal evidence also indicates that some terrorist groups may be engaged in wildlife crimes, particularly poaching, for monetary gain. Some observers claim that the participation of such actors in wildlife trafficking can therefore threaten the stability of countries, foster corruption, and encourage violence to protect the trade.

Reports of escalating exploitation of protected wildlife, coupled with the emerging prominence of highly organized and well-equipped illicit actors in wildlife trafficking, suggests that policy challenges persist. Commonly cited challenges include legal loopholes that allow poachers and traffickers to operate with impunity, gaps in foreign government capabilities to address smuggling problems, and persistent structural drivers such as lack of alternative livelihoods in source countries and consumer demand.

To address the illicit trade in endangered wildlife, the international community has established, through the Convention on International Trade in Endangered Species of Wild Fauna and Flora (CITES), a global policy framework to regulate and sometimes ban exports of selected species. Domestic, bilateral, regional, and global efforts are intended to support international goals of sustainable conservation, effective resource management, and enforcement of relevant laws and regulations.

Increased recognition of the potential consequences of wildlife trafficking has caused some observers and policymakers to question the efficacy of existing US and international responses and consider new options for addressing the problem. In November 2012, for example, then-Secretary of State Hillary Clinton announced the beginning of a revitalized effort to combat international wildlife trafficking. In July 2013, President Barack Obama issued Executive Order 13648 on Combating Wildlife Trafficking. The Executive Order identified poaching of protected species and the illegal trade in wildlife and their derivative parts and products as an escalating international crisis that is in the national interest of the United States to combat.

The US Congress has played a role in responding to these ongoing challenges and evaluating US policy to combat international wildlife trafficking. Over time, Congress has enacted a wide range of laws to authorize conservation programs, appropriate domestic and international funding for wildlife protection and natural resource capacity building, and target and dismantle wildlife trafficking operations. In recent years, Congress has also held hearings and events that have addressed the growing problem of wildlife crimes and raised key questions for next steps. Interest in wildlife crime may continue in the 113th Congress. Congressional activity may include evaluating the seriousness of the threat as a national security issue, as well as raising questions regarding the effectiveness of existing policies, ranging from biodiversity programs to anti-crime activities.

[…]

Introduction

Despite long-standing commitments to protect threatened species from overexploitation and to support natural resource management development, some argue that the scope and scale of illegal wildlife trade has risen to historic levels.[1] According to US government estimates, illegal trade in endangered wildlife products, including elephant ivory, rhino horns, and turtle shells, is worth at least an estimated $7 billion to $10 billion annually.[2] This figure does not include illegal logging and illegal fishing, which can account, respectively, for roughly an additional $30 billion to $100 billion annually and $10 billion to $23 billion annually.[3] Such figures may place illegal wildlife trafficking among the top 10 most lucrative criminal activities worldwide.

The continued existence of black markets for wild plants and animals is widely considered to be driven by ongoing consumer demand as well as gaps in natural resource management, law enforcement, and trade controls. Wildlife trafficking appears disproportionately to impact parts of the developing world that possess valuable natural resources, but do not have the capacity or political will to manage such resources transparently and effectively. Beyond its role in species extinction and endangerment, illegal wildlife trade has also been associated with the spread of disease and proliferation of invasive species.

Moreover, high prices for illegal wildlife, combined with often lax law enforcement and security measures, have motivated the involvement of transnational organized crime syndicates, who view such trafficking as an opportunity for large profits with a low risk of detection.[4] Even where heightened security measures to protect wildlife are implemented, they have not consistently had a deterrent effect. Instead, some wildlife trafficking operations have become more elaborate and, at times, more dangerous. Traffickers are known to employ sophisticated hardware for poaching operations, including night vision goggles, military-grade weapons, and helicopters. Park rangers have also been killed in the line of duty by poachers. Some shipments of the wildlife contraband and the illicit profits that result from such trafficking often involve circuitous routes, support from corrupt officials, a complex web of anonymous financial mechanisms, and broad networks of complicit middlemen, processors, exporters, and retailers along the transnational supply chain.[5]

[…]

Examples of Wildlife Crime

The following sections describe several illustrative forms of international illegal trade in wildlife, including trafficking in elephant ivory, rhino horn, caviar, and so-called bushmeat.

African Elephant Ivory

International trade in African elephants (Loxodonta africana) and their parts has been restricted under Appendix I since 1989, pursuant to CITES.[28] The 1989 CITES decision followed a decade of rampant ivory poaching that is estimated to have cut the total African elephant population to less than half its size in the late 1970s.[29] In the immediate years after the 1989 decision took effect, poaching appeared to drop significantly and African elephant populations in many parts of Sub-Saharan Africa began to recover.

Today, an estimated total of approximately 420,000 to 650,000 African elephants can be found in 37 countries in sub-Saharan Africa.[30] Elephant population trends, however, vary significantly by region, and the majority of known African elephants appear to be concentrated in Southern and Eastern Africa. Vibrant population growth primarily in Southern Africa has offset potentially large declines of forest elephants in Central Africa.[31] On the other hand, anecdotal indications of recent large-scale elephant killings suggest an uptick in poaching and a potential reversal of overall population trends.[32]

According to data compiled for the CITES-sponsored project Monitoring the Illegal Killing of Elephants (MIKE), poaching levels have increased since 2006. An estimated 17,000 elephants (range: 7,800 to 26,000) may have been illegally killed in 2011 at MIKE reporting sites in Africa—suggesting that the continental total of illegal killed elephants in 2011 was higher.[33] Early estimates for 2012 suggest that poachers may have killed more than 30,000 African elephants.[34]

[...]

Ivory seizure data collected by the Elephant Trade Information System (ETIS) reinforce claims that elephant poaching is increasing.[40] According to recent ETIS data, both the volume of illegally traded ivory as well as the number of large-scale illegal consignments trafficking internationally may be increasing. The increase in large-scale seizures, defined as consignments containing 800 kilograms of elephant ivory or more, is of particular concern to law enforcement officials, who suspect that well-organized criminal syndicates are likely involved in such movements. According to TRAFFIC International, there were 13 large-scale seizures of African elephant ivory in 2011 alone, likely representing some 2,500 elephants.[41]

Driving contemporary poaching is surging demand for ivory products in East Asia, where, historically, elephant ivory has long been valued for its cultural significance, as a symbol of status of wealth, and as an ingredient in the traditional treatment of certain types of health ailments.[42] China, in particular, has reportedly emerged as a major consumer of elephant ivory, driven in part by recent economic growth and the growing affluence of its citizens. Anecdotal reports suggest that Chinese expatriate communities working and living in Africa are playing a significant and perhaps growing role in elephant ivory smuggling. Asian criminal syndicates are reportedly involved in large-scale smuggling operations and may be collaborating with African criminal groups.

Rhino Horn

There are five living species of rhinoceros in the world, the survival of which are all threatened by over-hunting and habitat loss. Three species are native to Asia: the Sumatran rhino (Dicerorhinus sumatrensis), the Javan rhino (Rhinoceros sondaicus), and the

Indian rhino (Rhinoceros unicornis). Two species are native to Africa: the Black rhino (Diceros bicornis) and the White rhino (Ceratotherium simum). All five species have been subject to CITES trade prohibitions since the mid-1970s.[43] According to estimates by the International Union for the Conservation of Nature (IUCN) from 2012, there are approximately 140-210 Sumatran rhinos and 35-45 Javan rhinos remaining in the wild.[44] The last of the Vietnamese subspecies of the Javan rhino was shot in 2010 for its horn.[45] The Indian rhino, in contrast, is experiencing modest population growth, up to approximately 3,264 rhinos, due largely to strict protections by Indian, and more recently, Nepalese authorities. In the early 1900s, fewer than 200 Indian rhinos were believed to exist.

Despite redoubled conservation efforts initiated in the 1990s, surging demand in recent years for illegal rhino horn, particularly in Asian countries such as Vietnam, along with the corresponding increase in the involvement of organized international criminal syndicates in rhino horn smuggling, may imperil population gains made by African rhino species.[46] According to IUCN estimates from 2010, the African Black rhino population has increased to 4,880 since its nadir in 1995 of 2,410. The White rhino, whose population had been decimated to an estimated 20-50 surviving animals, has grown to approximately 20,165 in 2010.

[…]

Contemporary demand for rhino horn continues despite heighted rhino protection efforts, including GPS chipping and DNA tracking, as well as increased enforcement and penalties against perpetrators.[51] This surging demand originates primarily among consumers in Asia, who have reportedly driven the retail price of ground rhino horn to a height of as much as $20,000 to $30,000 per kilogram.[52] Such consumers seek rhino horn out as an ingredient in traditional remedies for fevers, headaches, and hangovers.[53] More recently, claims that rhino horn can cure cancer have further fueled demand.[54] Another consumer base for rhino horn emerged in Yemen, where ornate rhino-horn dagger handles have long been coveted among the elite.[55]

In total, one estimate indicates that more than 4,000 African rhino horns have been illegally sold in Asia between January 2009 and September 2012, amounting to some 12.6 tons of rhino horn available for purchase on the black market.[56] In contrast, some 3.1 tons of rhino horn were estimated to have been illegally sold between January 2006 and September 2009.[57]

Due in large part to its high black market prices, the illegal rhino horn trade has become one of the most structured wildlife crime activities, according to the CITES Secretariat. There are reportedly "clear indications" of highly organized, mobile, and well-financed criminal groups involved in both poaching and subsequent illegal trade of African rhino horn.[58] Observers suggest that criminal actors use sophisticated tools to poach rhinos, including helicopters, night-vision goggles, tranquillizer darts, and silenced heavy-caliber guns.[59] In addition to poaching, organized criminal groups have stolen rhino horns from government stocks, museums in Europe, private collections, antique dealers, auction houses, and taxidermists. Authorities in South Africa have documented evidence of suspected abuse of legal trophy hunting as a means to illicitly procure rhino horn for further black market sale.

[…]

Endnotes

1. International Conservation Caucus Foundation (ICCF), "The African Poaching Crisis," website, accessed Mar. 28, 2013, http://iccfoundation.us/index.php?option=com_content&view=article&id=445&Itemid=367.

2. State Department, "Secretary Clinton Hosts Wildlife Trafficking and Conservation," media note, Nov. 8, 2012. According to the National Intelligence Council, environmental crime, defined to include illegal wildlife trade, logging, trade in CFCs, and toxic waste dumping, generates an estimated $20 billion to $40 billion per year for transnational organized crime. See Office of the Director of National Intelligence, Special Report: The Threat to US National Security Posed by Transnational Organized Crime, 2011.

3. David J. Agnew et al., "Estimating the Worldwide Extent of Illegal Fishing," PLoS ONE 4(2), Feb. 2009; Christian Nellemann, ed. (INTERPOL and United Nations Environment Programme (UNEP)), Green Carbon, Black Trade, 2012.

4. World Wide Fund for Nature (WWF) and Dalberg, Fighting Illicit Wildlife Trafficking, 2012.

5. Vanda Felbab-Brown (Brookings), The Disappearing Act, Jun. 2011; World Bank, Going, Going, Gone, Jul. 2005.

28. African elephants were first designated in 1977 under Appendix II and then elevated to Appendix I in 1989. Pursuant to CITES provisions, specified trade in some African elephant ivory has been authorized. With appropriate documentation, pre-ban stocks may continue to be sold. On two occasions since 1989, the CITES Secretariat has supervised the legal international sale of ivory: once in 1999 (50 tons of ivory from Botswana, Namibia, and Zimbabwe were sold to Japan) and once in 2008 (108 tons of ivory from Botswana, Namibia, South Africa, and Zimbabwe were sold to Japan and China). For the purposes of noncommercial export of personal sport-hunted trophies, elephants may be taken in Botswana, Namibia, South Africa, and Zimbabwe; at the 14th meeting of the CITES Conference of the Parties (CoP14) in 2007, African countries committed to a nine-year moratorium on proposals to authorize ivory exports from populations listed under Appendix II. Domestic sales of ivory are not subject to CITES regulation.

29. In addition to poaching, elephant populations have been threatened by habitat loss due to human population growth and agricultural expansion.

30. African Elephant Database, 2012 Continental Totals, 2013; International Union for Conservation of Nature (IUCN) Red List of Threatened Species, Loxodonta africana, Feb. 2012; and IUCN, African Elephant Status Report 33, 2007.

31. According to a scientific journal article published in March 2013, the Central African forest elephant population is estimated to have declined by 62% from 2002 to 2011, with particularly severe declines noted among elephant populations located in DRC. Fiona Maisels et al., "Devastating Decline of Forest Elephants in Central Africa," PLoS ONE 8(3), Mar. 2013.

32. See also Margot Kiser, "The Economics of Extinction," The Daily Beast, Jan.29, 2013; "Tanzanian Parliament Calls for Stricter Anti-Poaching Measures," All Africa, Jan. 23, 2013; and Louis Kolumbia, "Bunge Team's Fury over Rise in Poaching," The Citizen (Tanzania), Jan. 22, 2013. "Brought to Tusk," Economist, Nov. 3, 2012; UNODC, "Environmental Crime," fact sheet, 2012, and Organized Crime and Instability in Central Africa, Oct. 2011.

33. CITES, Monitoring the Illegal Killing of Elephants, CoP16 Doc. 53.1, Nov. 30, 2012, and addendum, Feb. 19, 2013. For further discussion of the methodology, see Robert Burn et al., "Global Trends and Factors Associated with the Illegal Killing of Elephants," PLoS ONE 6(9), Sep. 2011.

34. See for example Wildlife Conservation Society estimates at http://www.wcs. org/elephants/. Another report estimates that as many as 50,000 elephants may be poached each year. See Navanti Group, Overview of Poaching and Armed Groups, Native Prospector (Central Bridge-LRA), DRC-04, Feb. 13, 2013 (UNCLASSIFIED//FOUO).

40. CITES, report of the Secretariat, Monitoring of Illegal Trade in Ivory and Other Elephant Specimens, CoP16 Doc. 53.2.1, Nov. 13, 2012, and ETIS Report of TRAFFIC, CoP16 Doc. 53.2.2 (Rev. 1), Feb. 8, 2013.

41. TRAFFIC, "2011: 'Annus Horribilis' for African Elephants, Says TRAFFIC," press release, Dec. 29, 2011. 42 See for example Bryan Christy, "Ivory Worship," National Geographic, Oct. 2012.

43. All rhino species are subject to the strictest bans on international trade (e.g., Appendix I), with the exception of White rhinos from South Africa and Swaziland, for which limited trade in live animals and export of hunting trophies is permitted pursuant to CITES.

44. CITES, report of the Secretariat, Rhinoceroses, CoP16 Doc. 54.2 (rev. 1), Jan. 10, 2013.

45. Sarah Brook et al. (WWF), Extinction of the Javan Rhinoceros (Rhinoceros sondaicus) from Vietnam, 2011.

46. CITES, report of the Secretariat, Rhinoceroses, CoP16 Doc. 54.2 (rev. 1), Jan. 10, 2013; Margot Kiser, "The Economics of Extinction" Newsweek, Jan. 25, 2013; "Poachers Prevail," Economist, May 12, 2012.

51. Mike Pflantz, "After Half-Century Absence, Black Rhinos Fly Home to Serengeti," Christian Science Monitor, May 21, 2010; "Getting Horny—Zimbabwe," Economist, Jul. 21, 2007.

52. UNODC, Environmental Crime, fact sheet, 2012. Other estimates suggest that rhino horn has retailed at $25,000 or $30,000 per pound. Another source reported that middlemen typically pay $3,500 per kilogram for rhino horn. See for example State Department (Hillary Rodham Clinton), "Remarks at the Partnership Meeting on Wildlife Trafficking," Nov. 8, 2012; Sharon Begley et al., "Extinction Trade," Newsweek, Mar. 10, 2008; Margot Kiser, "The Economics of Extinction," Newsweek, Jan. 25, 2013.

53. Tom Milliken and Jo Shaw (TRAFFIC), The South Africa—Viet Nam Rhino Horn Trade Nexus, Executive Summary, 2012; Nigel Leader-Williams, "Regulation and Protection," ch. 9 in Sara Oldfield, ed., The Trade in Wildlife (Sterling, VA: Earthscan, 2003); Geffrey Gettleman, "Coveting Horns, Ruthless Smugglers' Rings Put Rhinos in the Cross Hairs," New York Times, Jan. 1, 2013.

54. Kristin Nowell (TRAFFIC), report prepared for the CITES Secretariat, Assessment of Rhino Horn as a Traditional Medicine, SC62 Doc. 47.2 annex (rev.2), Apr. 2012.

55. "A Horny Headache," Economist, Nov. 20, 2010.

56. CITES, report of the Secretariat, Rhinoceros, CoP16 Doc. 54.2 (rev. 1), Jan. 10, 2013.

57. CITES, African and Asian Rhinoceroses—Status, Conservation and Trade, CoP15 Doc. 45.1 (rev. 1), annex, Nov. 20, 2009.

58. CITES, report of the Secretariat, Rhinoceros, CoP16 Doc. 54.2 (rev. 1), Jan. 10, 2013; TRAFFIC, "Rhinos in Crisis," press release, Jan. 15, 2013; Geffrey Gettleman, "Coveting Horns, Ruthless Smugglers' Rings Put Rhinos in the Cross Hairs," New York Times, Jan. 1, 2013.

59. "A Horny Headache," Economist, Nov. 20, 2010.

> "Widespread poverty, coupled
> with a lucrative overseas market
> for exotic animal products, have
> resulted in massive poaching of
> African and South-East Asian
> wildlife. In addition to the damage
> this causes to natural ecosystems, it
> also impacts on the tourism trade
> that comprises a key part of many
> national economies."

Environmental Crime Is Considered Transnational Organized Crime

United Nations Office on Drugs and Crime

Trafficking in wildlife and endangered species is no longer a local phenomenon. Because trafficking can generate large amounts of money, it has entered the realm of organized crime, especially in two specific locations with specific commodities: wildlife trafficking in Asia and Africa, and timber trafficking in Southeast Asia. In the following viewpoint, the United Nations gives specific examples of the types of trafficking and the resulting money made from commodities that are being trafficked by transnational groups operating illegally to harvest and sell them. The United Nations Office on Drugs and Crime (UNODC) helps make the world safer from drugs, organized crime, corruption, and terrorism.

From "Environmental Crime: Trafficking of Wildlife and Timber," United Nations Office on Drugs and Crime, ©2020 United Nations. Reprinted with the permission of the United Nations.

As you read, consider the following questions:

1. Why is illegal trafficking especially common in developing countries?
2. Why have crime organizations started participating in illegal trafficking?
3. What are some of the methods being used to try to stop this illegal trade? Does it seem realistic that they can decrease this activity?

Transnational organized crime is found wherever money can be made from illicit activities. One such activity is environmental crime, in particular trafficking in wildlife and timber. The problem is particularly acute in developing countries, where Governments often lack the capacity to regulate the exploitation of their natural resources. Poor management of natural resources can lead to corruption and even violent conflict.

Though environmental crime is a global and multifaceted phenomenon, this fact sheet deals with just two aspects of it in certain parts of the world: trafficking in wildlife from Africa and South-East Asia to other areas in Asia, and trafficking in timber from South-East Asia to the European Union and other areas in Asia. The illegal trade in timber between South-East Asia and the European Union and other areas in Asia was worth an estimated $3.5 billion in 2010.[1] By contrast, sales of elephant ivory, rhino horn and tiger parts in Asia were worth an estimated $75 million in 2010, but the environmental impact of this crime is much greater than the relatively small income it generates for criminals.

Trafficking in Wildlife from Africa and South-East Asia: Overview

Widespread poverty, coupled with a lucrative overseas market for exotic animal products, have resulted in massive poaching of African and South-East Asian wildlife. In addition to the damage this causes to natural ecosystems, it also impacts on the tourism trade that comprises a key part of many national economies.

Elephants, rhinos and tigers represent three of the biggest endangered species killed for their skins and/or bones. Ivory, rhino horn and tiger parts are among the most popular large animal "commodities" being trafficked from various parts of South-East Asia and Africa into Asia. There are also numerous smaller wild species that are harvested in South-East Asia for traditional medicine, food and decor products, as well as being captured live for the pet trade.

Trafficking in Wildlife from Africa and South-East Asia: The Involvement of Transnational Organized Crime Groups

Well-organized criminal groups have turned illicit environmental exploitation into a professional business with lucrative revenues leading to the exploitation of endangered and protected species in national parks. Every year, thousands of cases of poaching are reported by authorities in Africa and Asia. Representing just one incident, a reported 450 elephants were killed in early-2012 in the Bouba Ndjida National Park in northern Cameroon by poachers.[2]

Well-organized commercial ivory poachers are involved in the trade to, or through, many Asian countries. Between 1989 and 2009, there were at least 55 very large ivory seizures, with an average volume of 2.3 tons. In the destination markets, these shipments were worth about $2 million apiece at the wholesale level.[3]

Wildlife Trafficking: Flows and Prices

Elephants, rhinos and tigers are three of the best-known wildlife species that are killed for their body parts. Almost all ivory comes from African elephants and most of it is exported to Asia. Both African and Asian rhinos are targeted by poachers, and the few remaining tigers in the world, found in Asia, are hunted and killed for their body parts.

Elephants: In 2010, an estimated 7,500 elephants were killed, mostly in Central Africa. There are, on average, 92 ivory seizures per month, or about three per day.[4] While the price of ivory varies between countries, the total value of the ivory entering the global market is estimated at about $100 million a year. There are vast disparities between the prices paid in source countries and those paid in destination countries. While a kilogram of raw ivory sells for $15 in Africa, it can fetch about $850 in Asia. Value may also be added to the raw material if it is carved; the value of ivory objects cannot be gauged by their weight alone.[5]

Rhinos: After years of rhinos being killed for their horns, estimates place the world's wild rhino population at just 25,000.[6] Although seizures of rhino horn are generally smaller than those of elephant ivory, rhino horn is worth far more per kilogram. The illicit trade in rhino horn was worth about $8 million in 2010.[7] As with elephant ivory, prices paid in source countries may be as little as 1 per cent of the final retail price which, after the horn has been shaved or powdered for sale, has at times reached between $20,000 and $30,000 per kilogram.[8] South Africa is one of the countries most targeted by rhino poachers—in 2007, 13 rhinos were poached in the country; by 2011 this figure had jumped dramatically to 448, and numbers are expected to exceed 600 by the end of 2012.[9]

Tigers: Tiger parts continue to fetch high prices, with skins re- tailing for up to $20,000 in China, and raw bones selling for up to $1,200 per kilogram.[10] As all parts of the animal are sold, it is possible that many tigers are disappearing unnoticed. Based on reported poaching gures, however, this market is worth around $5 million per year.[11]

Trafficking in Wildlife from Africa to Asia

While poaching affects a number of African countries, some are affected much more than others. Central Africa is the main source of elephant ivory, while Southern Africa is targeted for rhino horn. Animal parts are illegally shipped or transported by air to Asia through a variety of routes, often concealed in legitimate cargo, with criminal syndicates taking advantage of the growing legal trade between Africa and Asia.

Trafficking in Wildlife Within Asia

Asia serves as a source, transit, and destination region for a large share of the endangered animals poached in the world, with Myanmar, the Lao People's Democratic Republic and Cambodia the most affected source countries. Cross-border wilder- ness areas represent a particularly vulnerable point for transnational trafficking. This, coupled with corruption, allows criminal networks to move illicitly harvested animals with relative ease.

Both tigers and rhinos are hunted and killed in Asia. There are now only around 3,200 tigers left in the wild, down from an estimated 100,000 at the beginning of the twentieth century,[12] and the poaching of these animals is a deliberate and systematic crime. There is evidence suggesting that poachers may be "commissioned" to hunt them. Asia is home to three of the world's five rhino species and their numbers have been reduced to such an extent that experts have warned that they may become extinct within the lifetime of the next generation.[13] In addition to these large animals, a variety of other wildlife species are targeted. Many die while being transported to destination countries.

Trafficking in Timber from South-East Asia: Overview

South-East Asia is home to some 7 per cent of the world's old-growth forests and many unique tree species. Regrettably, the region is experiencing the fastest deforestation rate on earth. Some of this deforestation is due to illicit logging, and in this way, organized crime contributes to irreversible environmental dam- age. Forests are critical in absorbing carbon from the atmosphere and this crime therefore has a global impact. Local communities are also affected through environmental damage, corruption of officials, violence and loss of income and livelihoods.

It is estimated that more than half of global demand for illicitly logged timber comes from Asia and Europe and that about 20 per cent of the global total of illegally felled timber is imported into the European Union, and about 25 per cent into China.[14]

Trafficking in Timber from South-East Asia: Corruption and the Involvement of Organized Crime Groups

Traffickers often rely on fraudulent paperwork to move illegal timber across borders. Methods used include fraudulently declaring a protected hardwood as an ordinary variety or falsifying certificates of origin, thereby declaring wood sourced in a protected area to be from an authorized source.

One of the repercussions of this illegal trade is the impact it has on corruption. In many instances, the paperwork needed to move illegal timber is not forged but rather bought from corrupt officials in timber source countries. Illegal logging gangs can also receive varying degrees of assistance from corrupt officials.

Trafficking in Timber from South-East Asia: Flows and Prices

Owing to its bulk, timber is generally transported by sea or by road and enters countries through official border crossings. Clandestine smuggling of timber is rare, and either fraudulent paperwork or bribery of customs officials is involved.

In the past, timber flows have mostly been illicit. For example, it was estimated that at one point in the first few years of the twenty-first century, 98 per cent of all the timber transported overland from Myanmar to China had been illegally logged. Similarly, at the height of the illegal logging problem in Indonesia, 80 per cent of the timber being transported out of the country had been illegally logged. At the time, the Government of Indonesia estimated that the illicit trade in timber was costing them $4 billion annually—five times more than the country's 2004 health budget. At its peak,

CHINA REVERSES BAN

China has reversed a decade old ban on using rhinoceros horns and tiger bones in medicine.

The law, which has been in place for 25 years, has now been altered so that the items can be obtained from farmed animals for use in "medical research or in healing".

The products are used in traditional Chinese medicine, despite a lack of evidence of their effectiveness in treating illness.

"Under the special circumstances, regulation on the sales and use of these products will be strengthened, and any related actions will be authorised, and the trade volume will be strictly controlled," the statement from the Chinese cabinet said.

No reason was given for the lifting of the ban, which was implemented in 1993 amid a global push to protect fast disappearing endangered species.

Environmentalists described the move as a significant setback for protecting the endangered animals.

The World Wildlife Fund (WWF) said the move to overturn the ban would have "devastating consequences globally" by allowing poachers and smugglers to hide behind legalised trade.

"With wild tiger and rhino populations at such low levels and facing numerous threats, legalised trade in their parts is simply too great a gamble for China to take," Margaret Kinnaird, WWF wildlife practice leader, said.

"This decision seems to contradict the leadership China has shown recently in tackling the illegal wildlife trade," she added.

Despite the previous ban, China has long allowed tiger farms to harvest the bones of dead animals.

Beijing has also tacitly allowed the sale of the bones for alleged medicinal purposes, according to a study by the Environmental Investigation Agency.

"China Reverses 25-Year Ban on Using Rhinoceros Horns and Tiger Bones in Medicine," by Shehab Khan, Independent Digital News and Media Limited, October 30, 2018.

deforestation was occurring at a rate of 2 million hectares a year—an amount equivalent to 300 football fields every hour.[15]

In 2010, an estimated 10 million cubic metres of illegally logged timber was imported into the European Union and China from South-East Asia, with an import value of roughly $3.5 billion.[16] Most of this was in the form of furniture and other finished products, but some was raw timber. The primary source of illicitly logged timber was Indonesia. Criminal groups often fraudulently label Indonesian wood as coming from Malaysia and trans-ship it from other parts of the region.

What Is Being Done?

Among the most influential of the many international conservation agreements that have been signed is the Convention on International Trade in Endangered Species of Wild Fauna and Flora (CITES), to which 175 States are parties. Under the Convention, States that do not take measures to protect endangered species are subject to escalating international pressure, which can ultimately result in trade sanctions.

The work of the United Nations Office on Drugs and Crime (UNODC) in countering environmental crime includes local, regional and global initiatives. The International Consortium on Combating Wildlife Crime (ICCWC), a partnership involving the CITES secretariat, the International Criminal Police Organization (INTERPOL), UNODC, the World Bank and the World Customs Organization, works to bring coordinated support to national wildlife law enforcement agencies and related subregional and regional networks. In mid-2012, UNODC, in partnership with other members of ICCWC, developed the Wildlife and Forest Crime Analytic Toolkit, which is aimed at assisting Governments in identifying the strengths and weaknesses of their criminal justice responses to wildlife and forest crime.

At the local and regional levels, UNODC works extensively to tackle various forms of environmental crime. In South-East Asia in particular, it conducts widespread research to better guide countries on countering trafficking in wildlife and illegal logging and encourages Governments to increase their efforts to protect natural resources and convict perpetrators of crimes against the environment. Critically, the work of UNODC in this area also involves working with authorities to improve laws and increase international cooperation to respond to crimes against the environment.

International NGOs such as WWF also play an important role in lobbying Governments for greater action against environmental crime and collaborating with them on conservation issues. They also build awareness among the general public at the global and local levels and lead debate on these concerns.

Aside from these international and national initiatives, the role of the public is essential. Here are some of the things that the public can do:

- Demand reduction. Consumers have a big—if not the biggest —role to play in stopping the illegal trade in wildlife and timber. As an informed consumer, you can help reduce demand by being aware of which species are under protection. This includes knowing whether products such as rhino horn or tiger bones are used in traditional medicine and paying careful attention to labelling when buying exotic timber.
- Eco-tourism. As a tourist, you can choose your routes, visits and destinations carefully and support eco-tourism. It should also be a given that you do not take home with you any animal or wildlife products—particularly not those discussed above.
- Publicity. High profile individuals can speak out against environmental crimes. In some countries, traditional practices and beliefs and a desire for status symbols hinder efforts to curb wildlife crime. Influential public voices can help to dispel myths, expose the cruelty of poaching and highlight the illegality of the practices involved, thereby building support for change.

- Awareness-raising. Lack of knowledge or awareness often leads to unknowing consumption of illegal wildlife products. Governments, NGOs and individuals can help spread information about these issues within society.
- Providing alternatives and sustainable livelihoods. As poverty is one of the main factors driving the illegal trade in wildlife, supporting legal income-generating activities can be an important measure, indirectly helping to curb environmental crime.
- Business. Companies can take action through smart and sustainable business decisions. In the timber trade in particular, companies should check certificates to ensure that products are of legal origin. If companies refuse to buy illegally produced timber and wood products, it will lead to less revenue for traffickers, and therefore less deforestation.

Disclaimer: This fact sheet has not been formally edited. The content of this fact sheet does not necessarily reflect the views or policies of UNODC or contributory organizations and neither does it imply any endorsement. The designations employed and the presentation of material in this fact sheet does not imply the expression of any opinion whatsoever on the part of UNODC concerning the legal status of any country, territory or city or its authorities, or concerning the delimitation of its frontiers and boundaries.

Endnotes

1. The Globalization of Crime: A Transnational Organized Crime Threat Assessment (United Nations publication, Sales No. E.10.IV.6). Available from www.unodc.org/documents/data-and-analysis/tocta/TOCTA_Report_2010_low_res.pdf.
2. Convention on International Trade in Endangered Species of Wild Fauna and Flora, "CITES Secretary-General expresses grave concern over reports of mass elephant killings in Cameroon", 28 February 2012. Available from www.cites.org/eng/news/pr/2012/20120228_elephant_cameroon.php.
3. The Globalization of Crime: A Transnational Organized Crime Threat Assessment.
4. Ibid.
5. Ibid.
6. John E. Scanlon, Secretary-General of the Convention on International Trade in Endangered Species of Wild Fauna and Flora, "Ivory and insecurity: the global

implications of poaching in Africa", written testimony to the United States of America Senate Foreign Relations Committee Hearing, Washington, D.C., 24 May 2012. Available from www.cites.org/eng/news/SG/2012/20120525_SG_US-Senate_testimony.php.

7. The Globalization of Crime: A Transnational Organized Crime Threat Assessment.
8. Ibid.
9. "Ivory and insecurity: the global implications of poaching in Africa".
10. The Globalization of Crime: A Transnational Organized Crime Threat Assessment.
11. Ibid.
12. Ibid.
13. "Ivory and insecurity: the global implications of poaching in Africa".
14. The Globalization of Crime: A Transnational Organized Crime Threat Assessment.
15. Ibid.
16. Ibid.

> "*Today there are people who hunt, and many more people who feel a deep-seated aversion to it; for whom the image of an animal slain by man—regardless of species, motive, legal status or even historical context—is nothing but repellent.*"

Inside the Minds of Trophy Hunters

Elle Hunt

Many people simply can't understand why anyone would want to hunt and kill a lion or one of many other species that are equally majestic. In the following excerpted viewpoint, Elle Hunt attempts to see from the perspective of trophy hunters, who are eager to kill animals such as lions or elephants. Hunters refer to "the complexity of the experience" of hunting that has little to do with the actual moment of killing, and that most people who have not been in Africa or on the ground with some of these species cannot understand the reality of wildlife management. Elle Hunt is a journalist whose work has appeared in the Guardian.

"Who Would Want to Kill a Lion? Inside the Minds of Trophy Hunters," by Elle Hunt, Guardian News and Media Limited, November 4, 2018. Reprinted by permission.

As you read, consider the following questions:

1. What does the media have to do with the reactions of people to trophy hunting? Are their assessments realistic or not?
2. What are some of the justifications given for trophy hunting?
3. What is meant by the "Hollywoodification" of wild animals? What would be an example of this?

The most elephants that Ron Thomson has ever killed by himself, in one go, is 32. It took him about 15 minutes. Growing up in Rhodesia, now Zimbabwe, Thomson began hunting as a teenager and quickly became expert. From 1959, he worked as a national parks ranger and was regularly called on to kill animals that came into conflict with man. "It was a great thrill to me, to be very honest," he says by phone from Kenton-on-Sea, the small coastal town in South Africa where he lives. "Some people enjoy hunting just as much as other people abhor it. I happened to enjoy it."

Now 79, Thomson has not shot an elephant for decades, and he struggles to find an open-minded audience for his stories of having, in his own words, "by far hunted more than any other man alive." Today there are people who hunt, and many more people who feel a deep-seated aversion to it; for whom the image of an animal slain by man—regardless of species, motive, legal status or even historical context—is nothing but repellent.

Today, these fault lines are most often exposed when a picture of a hunter grinning above their kill goes viral, as it did last month for the US hunter and television presenter Larysa Switlyk. Photographs of her posing with a goat and a sheep she had shot weeks earlier, and entirely legally, on the Scottish island of Islay went well beyond hunting circles on social media to be met with widespread disgust. Mike Russell, the local member of the Scottish parliament, told BBC Scotland it was unacceptable "to see people in camouflage … rejoicing at the killing of a goat."

Nicola Sturgeon publicly sympathised with the outcry and said the law would be reviewed. Switlyk posted on Instagram that she would be heading out of internet access on her "next hunting adventure." "Hopefully, that will give enough time for all the ignorant people out there sending me death threats to get educated on hunting and conservation."

And that was a goat. In the case of species that people travel to glimpse in the wild, or just watch on the Discovery Channel, the outrage can reverberate around the world. What would possess someone to want to kill these animals, let alone pay tens of thousands of pounds for the opportunity to do so?

"If you ask 100 hunters, you will get 100 different answers," says Jens Ulrik Høgh by phone from woodlands in Sweden, where he has been escorting groups on hunts of wild boar. Høgh, who works for Limpopo Travel & Diana Hunting Tours, a Danish hunting travel company, compares the attraction to that of mountaineering, scuba diving or golf: a physical hobby through which you can see the world. Hunters travel to experience different challenges. Zebras, for example, are tricky because they gather in herds out in the open and are watchful for predators. "There are always eyes looking in every direction—it typically takes a couple of days to get one." With baboons, numerous but intelligent primates, "you need to be a good hunter, a good stalker and a good shot."

The demand is reflected in the price tag. It costs relatively little—about £3,000—legally to hunt a giraffe because doing so is widely considered easy by hunters and therefore not desirable. "A giraffe is basically a very docile pile of meat. I could go shoot a cow in a field," says Høgh. (For the same reason, he tells me, he is rolling his eyes at Switlyk, the self-styled "hardcore huntress," posing with her trophies on Islay: "Who wants to kill a sheep?")

Although Høgh has made about 30 trips to Africa, he has never killed a lion, elephant or much "super-big game" for a straightforward reason: it is very expensive, typically upwards of £20,000. (And rightly so, he adds.) "I simply cannot afford to go lion hunting. But if I could, I would."

It is a tiny proportion of hunters who can, he says; he guesses fewer than 1%, although he is upfront about the distinction between hunting a wild lion and a "canned" one, an animal raised for slaughter. That comes much cheaper—but to hear Høgh tell it, it is a price no hunter with integrity would want to pay. "That's basically a farmed animal. You wouldn't even call it a hunt," he says.

One name keeps cropping up in conversations about so-called trophy hunting: Cecil, the lion killed by Minnesota dentist Walter Palmer in Zimbabwe in 2015. Although it was legal to shoot him, he had been lured out of a national park where he was well-beloved, and Palmer, hunting with a bow and arrow, did not kill Cecil outright, meaning the animal suffered. "It was an outrageous and shabby thing," says David Quammen, a US science writer who has written extensively about humanity's relationship with predators. But, he adds, there is a skill, even nobility, to hunting when "old-fashioned" rules of fair chase are observed. "Anyone who is not vegetarian is ill-advised to condescend to the people who do that."

It is undeniable that industrial meat production causes more global suffering than hunting. But even charges of hypocrisy do not deter opponents of hunting, even those who eat meat themselves, for whom the thrill of the chase could never justify taking a life.

This reflects the complexity of our often emotional, sometimes contradictory relationship with animals …. Large predators, such as big cats and bears, loom large in our collective consciousness, rendered either as "man-eaters" or charismatic and cuddly, like Simba and Pooh. And hunters argue sentiment is impeding our ability to protect them as a species.

"The 'Hollywoodification' of animals is, more than anything, the biggest threat to their survival," says Loodt Büchner. As director of Tootabi Hunting Safaris, outfitting mostly US clients on legal hunts of "50-plus species" on ranch land in five southern African countries, he is now mostly deskbound. But, growing up poor in South Africa, he came to hunting as a valuable source of protein, joining his father hunting for antelope when he was as young as five or six. Today, the philanthropic arm of his business provides schoolchildren in Eastern Cape province with 3,400 meals of trophy-hunted meat each month.

Büchner says most of the backlash to hunting comes from "very fragile people" who conflate wildlife conservation—which can sometimes necessitate killing—with preservation, "shooting with a Canon camera, not a rifle."

He makes no distinction between people who hunt for food and those who pay his company $13,500 (£10,400) for a package of 10 "trophy animals" in 10 days. Regardless of circumstance, no animal killed is ever wasted, with the meat either sold or consumed. In fact, he says, Tootabi has seen a 54% increase in revenue that he credits to the killing of Cecil because, before then, people didn't know legal hunting was possible. Conversely, Høgh suggests the increase might instead be the result of the subsequent crackdown on canned lion hunting.

Much of the interest is from recent university graduates, says Büchner, which he ascribes to their generation's desire to document unique experiences on social media. "It's amazing to see the number of young people in Manhattan who all of a sudden realise there's a world out there, that it's not just shares and stocks: 'We could actually go hunt animals, it sounds amazing.'"

[…]

For Høgh, the trouble is that non-hunters see the act of killing an "innocent" animal as fundamentally dramatic or evil, as well as the primary goal of hunting. "It's not about those 0.5 seconds," he says. "I've met extremely few who took pleasure in killing animals, and the ones I have met, I wish they would actually stop hunting. It's just perverse—they're sadists."

But it is entirely understandable people would assume otherwise, he adds, when that is what gets documented. "Hunters have been very poor at communicating the complexity of the experience. Often what we show the world is a picture of a dead animal and us sitting behind it with a big grin on our face."

Høgh asks his groups not to post photos of their kills online, or at least to be mindful of how they might strike a non-hunter.

But there are individuals—he assumes an American accent—who demand that it is "their right." "And it is their right. But it's still damn stupid."

To add to the complexity of the debate, some point out that many of the people who most oppose the hunting of animals will never know the realities, and sometimes the costs, of living alongside them. "Wildlife is a problem for many people," says Prof Adam Hart, a scientist at the University of Gloucestershire and host of the 2015 BBC Radio 4 documentary Big Game Theory. Elephants, for instance, raid crops and damage trees. Big cats kill livestock, while impala compete with them for food.

There is an important distinction, Gonçalves says, between an individual who kills an animal sensitively and skilfully for meat that they will consume themselves—"and hunting for a plaque on the wall and a selfie."

Many, including Hart and Büchner, believe that hunting even big game can be not only sustainable but beneficial to species' survival. They call it the "if it pays, it stays" approach, meaning that, by putting a monetary figure on animals, they become valuable and worthy of preservation. They say that if hunting and ranging is more lucrative than farming livestock or ecotourism, landowners are incentivised to buy more land—thereby conserving habitat—and ensure species' long-term survival.

Hart says figures from Namibia and South Africa seem to bear this out, but cautions against oversimplification. "Is it good where we've got a system whereby the only way we can conserve wildlife is to actively use it? We [Britons] would say no, but we have a very privileged viewpoint. The biggest problem is that people don't understand the complexities of the situation—there are different species, different habitats, different countries, different economies, different societies."

Not even Packer is against lion hunting in principle. But in Tanzania he found that the industry was resistant to reform and charging far too little per hunted animal to fund the conservation of their land. "What's really infuriating to me is that they're posing like they are the great saviours of wildlife, but they're putting in pennies where they should be putting in pounds."

A fair price, Packer says, would be about $1m a lion. "Steve Chancellor may be able to afford it. But there aren't many Steve Chancellors."

In Botswana, home to the world's largest elephant population, Hart says that numbers have grown so great that their habitat cannot support them and they are causing lasting damage. The government there is considering lifting a 2014 ban on hunting elephants for sport, pointing to figures that say there are 237,000 animals in an area able to support 50,000.

Last Monday, Sir Ranulph Fiennes, Bill Oddie, Peter Egan, a cross-party group of MPs and a lifesize inflatable elephant delivered a 250,000-strong petition against the proposal to lift the ban to the Botswana high commission in London, saying that allowing hunting could push the species towards extinction. The protest marked the launch of the Campaign to Ban Trophy Hunting, founded by Eduardo Gonçalves, the former CEO of the League Against Animal Sports. He says elephant numbers in Botswana have only increased as a result of the 2014 ban, while populations in neighboring countries have declined. "The ban on trophy hunting has been good for conservation—there's no two ways about it," he says.

He is scathing of the justification that hunting benefits communities or conservation, pointing out that if that was their motivation, hunters could donate direct to the cause. "They try to come up with rational arguments to justify their bloodlust," he says. Moreover, he adds, there is an "indivisible line" between trophy hunting and poaching, with laws against poachers having an impact on poor African people while wealthy westerners lawfully carry out the same practice, for a price.

Thomson says many species suffer when there is an excess of elephants: arboreal snakes and chameleons, black hornbills, martial eagles, bush babies ("beautiful little monkey-like things"). Elephants' lives have been valued above theirs by "purely human sentiment", he says, now audibly angry. "The people who think like that don't know anything about wildlife management. These are people who have never left their armchairs, in London or New York or wherever they live. They make these demands, and they haven't a clue what is going on. We are the ones looking after the elephants in Africa. They are the ones that are causing all the problems."

[…]

> *"Anyone who spends time in the woods and watches wildlife would demand that we do more work on improving habitat."*

There Is No Sport in Canned Hunting

Oliver Milman

In the following viewpoint, Oliver Milman compares "canned hunts" where hunters can easily kill trophy animals, with hunting that takes place in the wild and involves careful tracking and skillful shooting. The author uses the example of Theodore Roosevelt and the hunting culture he modeled, but also the social media reactions to the killing of a well-loved lion named Cecil by a trophy hunter. He concludes with the current example of President Donald Trump's son, who is trying to recreate a hunting culture in the United States. Oliver Milman is an environmental reporter for Guardian US.

As you read, consider the following questions:

1. What is the "deepening divide" within the hunting community?
2. How is the hunting culture an example of male bonding?
3. Does the author seem to present an opinion of his own stance on hunting?

"'There's No Sport in That': Trophy Hunters and the Masters of The Universe," by Oliver Milman, Guardian News and Media Limited, July 27, 2017. Reprinted by permission.

They're known as canned hunts; captive mammal hunting ranches in the US which offer the chance to shoot a zebra or antelope or even a lion for several thousand dollars. The animals are fenced in and often unafraid of humans so the kills are easy, to the extent that some venues even provide the option of shooting them via the internet, with the use of a camera and a gun on a mount.

It's estimated that there are more than 1,000 of them—completely legal. But many US hunters consider them a betrayal of every belief they hold dear. "I don't consider that hunting," said John Rogalo, a New Jersey hunter who has been stalking bears, deer and turkeys for nearly 50 years. "It's a weird culture that has developed in this country in the past few years. I joke that you may as well ask the farmer if you could shoot his black Angus because at least you'd get more meat for it."

Rogalo is firmly on one side of an ever-deepening divide in the hunting community—one of the longest and proudest traditions in US culture. He considers himself part of a proud lineage of conservation-minded hunters whose totem is Theodore Roosevelt, the former president and avid outdoorsman. Roosevelt and his contemporaries invoked a mantra of "fair chase" which they defined as an "ethical, sportsmanlike and lawful" pursuit that does not give the hunter some sort of improper advantage over the prey. He would call himself a true "hunter".

"Hunters view it as a sport, you may take days or weeks tracking your quarry ... If you didn't get anything, that didn't matter. It was the pursuit that counts," says Craig Packer, a zoologist best known for his work on lions in south and east Africa. On the other side of the divide from Rogalo are the "shooters", as they are known. "The shooter will come over, check his Blackberry every few hours, kill something and go home. There are now more and more shooters—younger, more urban, masters of the universe. They will have bait put out, sit in a blind and shoot lions as they feed. There's no sport in that. It's like a selfie."

Walter Palmer, the Minnesota dentist who gained international infamy after shooting Cecil the lion in 2015, would almost certainly

SOCIAL MEDIA LAMBASTES
A TROPHY HUNTER

A trophy hunter who is believed to have lured a lion to its death at the Kruger National Park has been identified on social media as a wealthy American from Kentucky, who is facing a harsh social media backlash.

The social media justice Jared Whitworth has faced so far has included the sharing of his cellphone number and email address, along with vilification, outrage and threats.

The trophy hunter was alleged to have paid £60 000 (or more than a million rand) for the controversial kill, and kept the lion's skin and head as trophies.

The South African professional hunter who reportedly organised the shoot, Graham Sales, is facing a much smaller, but still significant, backlash.

Conservationists fear the lion was a dominant male called Skye, the leader of the park's western pride, who has not been seen since the hunt.

African Geographic reported the trophy hunting team had denied this, claiming the slain animal was in fact an old male lion with worn

qualify as a shooter rather than a hunter. Palmer paid guides $50,000 to stalk Cecil, famed for his black mane, before shooting him with a bow and arrow. Controversially, bait was used to lure the 13-year-old lion outside of a protected area in Zimbabwe.

Palmer was initially apologetic for killing a famous and well-loved lion but has since adopted the mantra that the fee he paid will help lion conservation in Africa, recently tweeting that "trophy hunting actually HELPS." Palmer is a member of "hunter's rights" organisation the Safari Club, which has logged more than 40 of Palmer's kills including, among other animals, a polar bear.

Last week it was revealed that Cecil's six-year-old son Xanda was shot and killed by another trophy hunter, also outside the boundary of a reserve in Zimbabwe. It's unclear what will happen teeth and a protruding spine. However, they refused to provide a photo of the dead lion to prove their claim, citing legal and personal safety concerns.

Canned lion hunters are never popular on social media, with some believing the backlash against identified culprits could lead to the "sport" being banned.

In 2015, a Minnesota dentist called Walter Palmer faced a massive backlash after he killed Cecil, a beloved lion who was a major attraction at the Hwange National Park in Zimbabwe.

After Palmer was named as the hunter who killed Cecil, his dentist practice at the Bloomington clinic and Eden Prairie home became the focus of protests. Animal welfare groups also vandalised a holiday home Palmer owns in Florida.

The clinic was shut for weeks, eventually reopening without him.

New details emerged earlier this year that Cecil the Lion's killers lured him out of a protected park in Zimbabwe with an elephant carcass, causing renewed outrage.

Palmer was never prosecuted for the killing of Cecil.

"Trophy Hunter Shamed and Threatened on Social Media," The Citizen, November 7, 2018.

to Xanda's remains—Palmer had wanted to sever and mount Cecil's head before it was handed over to police—but these trophies are garnered with minimum effort essentially for the thrill of it, all to a backdrop of a 60% decline in African lion numbers over the past three decades.

Most US hunters remain on the "hunting" side of the debate. A nationwide poll from 2013 found that 35% of American hunters aged over 18 said they hunted "for meat" with just 1% saying they wanted to procure a trophy from the animal, but tightly-held tradition and socialising are also key elements of the American hunting experience.

"A lot of it is about storytelling and male bonding. There is a lot of card playing," Simon Bronner, an ethnologist who has spent plenty of time with hunters in Pennsylvania while researching books said. "There's this idea that being out in the woods is recreating the pioneer experience that they see as being the basis of America. They are living an experience where land is a resource controlled locally in an urbanized country that is changing around them."

It's the emotional charge, the quiet time in the woods (many hunters frown upon cellphone use and reject mechanized modern weaponry in favor of bows and muskets) that creates a virtuous circle, according to Bronner, that brings revenue and oversight to states through licenses while ensuring the stewardship of the land. "Anyone who spends time in the woods and watches wildlife would demand that we do more work on improving habitat."

The Original Hunter-Conservationist

Theodore Roosevelt, the 26th president of the United States, perfectly embodied the belief that "true hunting" was a vital part of conservation.

Up until the end of the 19th century, it had been open season on American wildlife. Bison were considered so bountiful that people could shoot them from trains, while waterfowl were gunned down to provide plumage for hats.

But at the turn of the century nascent environment groups such as the Audubon Society, as well as a new breed of venerated "gentleman" hunters such as Roosevelt, Davy Crockett and Daniel Boone—the Boone and Crockett club exists to this day—pushed for change.

Roosevelt didn't create the first national park—Yellowstone, perhaps the first reserve of its kind in the world, was established in 1872 under president Ulysses S Grant—but it was he who set out the moral imperative of protected areas for America's natural wonders.

Even as he was heading west in order to hunt the continent's big game before it disappeared, Roosevelt's writing was pockmarked with sadness at the disappearing bounty. He wrote timelessly that it is "vandalism wantonly to destroy or to permit the destruction of what is beautiful in nature, whether it be a cliff, a forest, or a species of mammal or bird.

"Here in the United States we turn our rivers and streams into sewers and dumping-grounds, we pollute the air, we destroy forests, and exterminate fishes, birds and mammals."

As president, Roosevelt signed five national parks into existence and helped create the Antiquities Act, which allows presidents to unilaterally designate protected areas—which he used 18 times, most notably to safeguard the Grand Canyon.

Simultaneously his presidency spawned the US Forest Service to protect public lands where hunting, grazing and other activities are allowed, unlike in the more sacrosanct national parks. He helped draw the clear delineation between pristine areas almost frozen in time for species conservation, and areas for fishing and shooting and rampaging around on horses and, later, four wheel drive cars; a distinction that has endured in conservation management around the world. This sort of neatly divided mapping is by no means perfect—Cecil the lion didn't know he had crossed an invisible line to an unprotected area; elephants will never have their long migration routes free of farmland and therefore irate farmers—but it at least fostered the idea that wildlife had a place too, that animals don't actually provide an inexhaustible supply of targets for carefree hunters.

But even as he made these reforms, Roosevelt continued to embrace the American ideal of hunting as an activity for all. His great grandson Tweed Roosevelt says: "Hunting for Brits was an upper class activity, whereas we've gone to great lengths to make it an activity for the people... Sportsmen like Roosevelt created a concept of fair chase, rather than firing cannons at ducks. I don't think he would support canned hunts."

But Roosevelt was also a keen, even obsessive, hunter, and saw no conflict in that: "Nothing adds more to a hall or a room than fine antlers when their owner has been shot by the hunter-displayer, but always there is an element of the absurd in a room furnished with trophies of the chase that the displayer has acquired by purchase," he wrote in 1902. Two weeks after he finished his second term in the White House, Roosevelt embarked upon a 15 month shooting tour with the goal of bringing back a cornucopia of African wildlife to start a natural history museum in Washington DC. The former president and his entourage bagged thousands of animals, including a bull rhino in the Belgian Congo: he called the beast "a monster surviving over from the world's past, from the days when the beasts of the prime ran riot in their strength, before man grew so cunning of brain and hand as to master them."

Even then, Roosevelt's huge kills sparked some public protest. These days, despite the claims by hunters that their money helps local communities and species, there is growing revulsion against the idea of big game hunting. There was barely constrained glee recently when Theunis Botha, a South African big game hunter, died recently after being crushed by an elephant that had been shot by a colleague.

An online petition mourning the elephant calls the incident "karma". And palpable anger at Cecil's death forced Palmer into hiding, a fate shared by Texas millionaire Corey Knowlton, who paid $350,000 at an auction for the privilege of shooting an endangered black rhino in Namibia in 2015. Knowlton said the three-day hunt would benefit the species but then faced death threats over his trip, and told CNN, which had accompanied him on the safari: "I think people have a problem just with the fact that I like to hunt. Being on this hunt, with the amount of criticism it brought and the amount of praise it brought from both sides, I don't think it could have brought more awareness to the black rhino."

Then there is the Trump family, breezily upending norms and expectations.

Donald Trump Jr., the president's eldest son, goes hunting with his bow most weekends and is referred to by his friends as the "Fifth Avenue redneck." He has targeted elk and mule deer at home as well as "15 or 16 species" in Africa, where he has been pictured grasping a severed elephant's tail and holding a dead leopard with his brother, Eric.

Last year, Donald Trump Jnr said the US Fish and Wildlife Service (USFWS) "should be encouraging American hunters legally and ethically hunting abroad, not hindering them." He also called for wolves to be culled in the US west, claiming they deprive hunters of moose.

Junior is seemingly attempting to fashion a new type of "hunter"—invoking the spirit of Roosevelt while posing with big game body parts and viewing public lands as sites for shooting and mining and not much else.

"We have to make sure we're heard," he told Petersen's Hunting. "Lately, we've been a forgotten group. I want to change that now and forever.

"And we are going to do whatever we can to make sure that any kind of Trump presidency is going to be the best since Theodore Roosevelt for outdoorsmen, for hunters, for our public lands, and for this country as it relates to anything in the great outdoors."

Periodical and Internet Sources Bibliography

The following articles have been selected to supplement the diverse views presented in this chapter.

BBC News, "When Is It Hunting and When Is It Poaching?" July 29, 2015. https://www.bbc.com/news/world-africa-33699347

Nicole Blanchard, "Sharing the Culture of Hunting with a Younger Generation." Associated Press, February 9, 2019. https://apnews.com/1100307c3acb4a42a0d820a5562db94a

Patrick Blanchfield, "What Makes Hunting So Divisive." New Republic, August 23, 2018. https://newrepublic.com/article/150848/makes-hunting-divisive

Benajmin Durr, "Conservationists Take Aim at Poachers." Africa Renewal/United Nations, May–July 2017. https://www.un.org/africarenewal/magazine/may-july-2017/conservationists-take-aim-poachers

Got Hunts.com, "Importance of America's Hunting Culture." https://gothunts.com/the-importance-of-maintaining-americas-hunting-culture

In Defense of Animals, "Hunting—The Murderous Business." 2019. https://www.idausa.org/campaign/wild-animals-and-habitats/hunting

Vern Loomis, "Why We Kill and Hunt." Center for Humans and Nature. https://www.humansandnature.org/does-hunting-make-us-human-why-we-kill-and-hunt

Dr. Cameron K. Murray, "The Lion's Share? On the Economic Benefits of Trophy Hunting." Conservation Action Trust, February 2017. https://conservationaction.co.za/resources/reports/lions-share-economic-benefits-trophy-hunting

Manish Pandey, "Scientists: Banning Trophy Hunting 'Doesn't Protect Animals.'" BBC News, August 30, 2019. https://www.bbc.com/news/newsbeat-49524189

Amanda Paulsen, "How China's Loosening of Rhino, Tiger Ban Could Spur Poaching." *Christian Science Monitor*, November 9, 2018. https://www.csmonitor.com/Environment/2018/1109/How-China-s-loosening-of-rhino-tiger-ban-could-spur-poaching

Julian Rademeyer, "Fact Sheet: How Much Does Hunting Contribute to African Economies?" Africa Check, September 16, 2015. https://africacheck.org/factsheets/factsheet-how-much-does-hunting-contribute-to-african-economies

Niki Rust, "Trophy Hunting Is Not Poaching and Can Help Conserve Wildlife." The Conversation.com, August 14, 2014. http://theconversation.com/trophy-hunting-is-not-poaching-and-can-help-conserve-wildlife-29938

Em Steck, "How America's Hunting Culture Shaped Masculinity, Environmentalism, and the NRA." Vox, June 12, 2018. https://www.vox.com/conversations/2018/6/12/17449154/hunting-culture-shaped-masculinity-the-nra-and-environmentalism

Soňa Supeková, "Hunting Traditions in Europe—The Way of Life for Hunters." Center for Humans and Nature. https://www.humansandnature.org/hunting-sona-supekova

Mindy Weisberger, "Hunting Big Game: Why People Kill Animals for Fun." Live Science, May 24, 2017. https://www.livescience.com/59229-why-hunt-for-sport.html

CHAPTER 3

Does Hunting Increase the Risk of Extinction?

Chapter Preface

In most places around the globe, it is not easy to be an animal now. Climate change is altering habitats and environments, shifting weather patterns, and creating food instability among humans that leads them to seek new food sources, including animals.

In addition to these factors that are creating stress in animal populations and edging many species toward extinction, there is a great deal of arguing between hunters and nonhunters as to whether hunting is also pushing species—especially big game or trophy animals—to extinction.

Throughout American history, there have been animals that became extinct because of overhunting. The great auk, the passenger pigeon, and the heath hen are just a few examples. Some animals, like the American bison, were pushed to the brink of extinction by large scale hunting and have only recovered in the last few decades. The Endangered Species Act, passed in 1973, was intended to conserve threatened and endangered plants and animals as well as the habitats in which they lived. This law forced federal agencies

> to ensure that actions they authorize, fund, or carry out are not likely to jeopardize the continued existence of any listed species or result in the destruction or adverse modification of designated critical habitat of such species. The law also prohibits any action that causes a "taking" of any listed species of endangered fish or wildlife. Likewise, import, export, interstate, and foreign commerce of listed species are all generally prohibited.[1]

However, the law has not stopped hunters from killing threatened or endangered animals, often because they cannot correctly identify what species of animal they are targeting, especially in low-light conditions like sunrise and dusk. Some animal rights supporters claim that the law makes no difference to hunters who might be intoxicated or using illegal weapons and tactics to attract and kill animals.

Hunters and hunting organizations argue that hunters are a valuable asset in the control of animal populations, and in culling smaller or unhealthy animals so that their genes are not carried on through breeding, weakening the species. However, as climate change stresses animal populations and human need for food alike, the protection of endangered animals will become an increasingly contentious issue.

Endnotes

1. "Summary of the Endangered Species Act." United States Environmental Protection Agency, accessed December 27, 2019. https://www.epa.gov/laws-regulations/summary-endangered-species-act

> *"It's not just humans who want to shoot something. More often it's organized criminals who want to cut up animals and sell them to different humans who think they'll make them live longer or look good on a wall. Other times it's impoverished people looking for ready cash, or even a meal."*

Poachers Are Moving Some Animals Toward Extinction

Jessica Phelan

The killing of a popular lion in Zimbabwe has been the catalyst for many protests about trophy hunting and endangered animals. In the following viewpoint, Jessica Phelan lists six animals that are currently endangered, and why they have become threatened. The author argues that animals aren't simply becoming extinct because of human hunting, but because of organized crime members or because of people who are starving and simply need to eat. Endangered animals are under attack for a variety of reasons. Jessica Phelan is a web and radio journalist and is former editor of GlobalPost Morning Chatter.

"6 Endangered Animals That Poaching Might Take from Us Forever," by Jessica Phelan, Public Radio International, July 31, 2015. Reprinted by permission.

As you read, consider the following questions:

1. How does the author's tone affect the content of the article? Does it make the article stronger or weaker?
2. Identify one of the major reasons why endangered animals are sought by poachers and organized crime.
3. What is the author hoping to convey with her very last sentence in this article?

D o you want the bad news or the even worse news? The bad news you probably already know: Cecil the lion, one of Zimbabwe's best loved wild animals, was slain last week at the hands of unscrupulous safari guides and, it's claimed, a crossbow-happy dentist from Minnesota.

Cecil's death, sadly, is only the tip of the iceberg—and unlike the real icebergs we're so intent on melting, this one ain't shrinking, it's growing. Each year humans deliberately kill thousands of the animals we're privileged to share the planet with, even the ones we nominally call "protected." Not content with destroying their habitats and compromising their food supply, some members of our species hunt and slaughter creatures that are already struggling to survive.

It's not just humans who want to shoot something. More often it's organized criminals who want to cut up animals and sell them to different humans who think they'll make them live longer or look good on a wall. Other times it's impoverished people looking for ready cash, or even a meal.

Whatever poachers' motivations, they're threatening to wipe some of the most vulnerable species off the face of the earth. Here are six animals that, like Cecil, poaching might rob us of forever.

1. Elephants

Right now, poachers are the single biggest threat to elephants' survival. After decades of decimation of elephant populations for their ivory, the international trade in "white gold" was banned in 1989. Yet people's persistent willingness to hand over bigger and bigger sums of money for dead elephant tusk—in China, $2,100 per kilo on average as of last year—has made it more tempting than ever for profit seekers to kill elephants illegally. The most comprehensive survey to date stated that 100,000 African elephants were poached across the continent between 2010 and 2012. According to those figures, in 2011 alone poachers killed roughly one in every 12 African elephants.

Sometimes elephant poachers, like Cecil the lion's killers, use bows and arrows as their weapon of choice. Sometimes they tip the arrows with poison, like the people who last year slaughtered one of Kenya's most famous elephants, Satao, and hacked off his magnificent 6.5-foot tusks. Other hunting expeditions have seen gangs turn grenades and AK-47s on entire herds, even within the supposed shelter of national parks.

Asian elephants, considered an even more vulnerable species, are also hunted for their tusks, body parts, meat and hide. Unlike their African cousins, only male Asian elephants have tusks—a fact that makes the consequences of poaching even more devastating, since the selective killings of bulls creates a gender imbalance and thereby reduces reproduction in the remaining population.

2. Rhinos

Rhinoceroses, like elephants, suffer the misfortune of having an external protrusion that humans arbitrarily place a crazily high value upon. Crazy, crazy high: rhino horn was reported to be selling for $65,000 per kilo in 2012, making it more expensive by weight than gold, diamonds or cocaine.

The demand comes from Southeast Asia, particularly Vietnam, where some people believe that consuming rhino horn—approximate nutritional value: human fingernails—will cure everything from cancer to hangovers to a dull night out. The black market demand for rhino horn has led to a surge in poaching of the critically endangered black rhino and the more numerous southern white rhino across southern Africa since 2008.

This is especially the case in South Africa, where illegal killings hit another record high this year at 393 in the 12 months till April. And that's not counting legal deaths. Trophy hunters can pay more than $100,000 for the "right" to kill a rhino and keep its horn, under a government scheme that allows hunters to shoot one rhino a year with the proper permit. Many suspect it's open to abuse by people who've come for the horn, not the hunt. Either way, the rhino ends up dead.

Finding themselves faced with more and more mutilated rhino carcasses, horns hacked off sometimes while the animals were still alive, authorities are resorting to increasingly drastic methods to try and protect the rhinos that remain, from drone surveillance to a rhino DNA database to even poisoning rhinos' horns. So far, it's not working. The western black rhinoceros went extinct in 2011. The rest of Africa's wild rhinos could follow suit within 20 years.

3. Tigers

Fact: humans are the worst thing ever to happen to tigers. We'd hunted them down to just 5,000 and 7,000 individuals worldwide by the late 1990s. That was considered a dangerously low number then. By 2014, it had halved. Some estimates say fewer than 2,500 mature tigers currently exist in the wild.

The problem is our passion for every part of them: Tiger skins, bones, teeth, claws, tails and even whiskers find a place on the black market as decorative items or ingredients in traditional Asian remedies. The illegal trade is further fuelled by tiger farms in China and Vietnam, where large numbers of the animals are bred for their body parts. Depressingly, as many as three times more tigers exist on such farms than in the wild. Elsewhere, tigers are reared to be killed in "canned" hunts by trophy seekers.

Even in the wild, we're killing tigers faster than we can destroy their habitat. The most haunting proof that poaching is the greatest threat to tigers? "Empty forest syndrome": Roughly 620,000 square miles of what should be tiger habitat currently lies unoccupied.

4. Sea Turtles

Don't imagine that poachers only ransack the land. Oh no, they find plenty to kill in the sea, too. One of their most popular targets is the hawksbill, the tropical turtle whose beautiful yellow-and-brown shell provides the commodity known as tortoiseshell. Millions of the animals have been killed over the past century to feed the fashion for tortoiseshell jewelry, glasses, ornaments, instruments and other items, with the result that the species is now critically endangered. The international trade has been banned for almost 40 years, but a black market continues to thrive in Asia, notably China and Japan, and in the Americas.

Hawksbills are also killed for what's under their shell—their meat. Either it's eaten by humans, or used as bait to catch sharks. Other parts of their body are used to make leather, perfume and cosmetics, or stuffed whole and displayed as "decoration."

For all sea turtles, including the leatherbacks and green turtles that also find themselves on the receiving end of poachers' deadly attention, poaching is potentially catastrophic. The animals take so long to reach breeding age—more than 30 years, in some cases—that many are killed before they ever have the chance to reproduce.

5. Lemurs

There are no mammals on earth more endangered than lemurs—and yet, we're still hunting them. Over 90 percent of all species of the big-eyed primates—found only on the island of Madagascar—are considered vulnerable, endangered or critically endangered.

Deforestation and climate change are largely to blame for their decline. But hunting lemurs for their meat, which has reportedly increased in the chaos that followed Madagascar's 2009 coup, is also diminishing their tiny numbers. Despite legislation that makes killing them illegal, lemurs are poached either to be sold to restaurants or simply to be eaten by impoverished locals desperate for food.

The tragic irony is that a lemur in the hand is worth much less than two in the bush. Like lions in Zimbabwe, lemurs are a huge tourism attraction for Madagascar and will always make more profit for more people alive than dead. Not to mention the fact that NO ONE SHOULD BE KILLING LEMURS ANYWAY.

6. Gorillas

Still clinging on to a scrap of faith in humanity? Prepare to drop it, quick. We humans are slaughtering the greatest of our fellow great apes, the gorilla.

Gorillas used to be protected from our murderous appetite by the huge tracts of unspoiled forest in Central Africa that they lived in. But then—oopsy!—we spoiled it. Logging, new roads and the migrations caused by successive wars brought people within firing range of gorillas. You can guess what happened next. What began as subsistence hunting quickly grew into an illicit commercial trade in gorilla meat that sees the animals butchered, transported and sold on. An increasing number of them make it as far as cities, where restaurants serve up "bushmeat" to wealthy clientele who like their dinner endangered.

If that weren't enough, poachers have begun to target gorillas for their body parts, to be used in folk remedies or simply as trophies. Heads, hands and feet are said to be particularly popular.

Other gorillas are casualties of other crimes in their protected habitat. In the Democratic Republic of Congo's historic Virunga National Park, mountain gorillas have been found shot through the back of the head, execution-style, in attacks blamed on traders who illegally harvest wood to make charcoal from the protected forest.

All species of gorilla are suffering, including the critically endangered western lowland gorilla. Combined with habitat loss, climate change and disease, numbers are now so low and reproduction so limited that the deaths of even a few animals at the hands of poachers stand to have a major impact on the population. According to the International Union for Conservation of Nature, by the middle of this century we may well have wiped out more than 80 percent of all western gorillas in just three generations.

Good job, humankind.

> "No native vertebrate species in the eastern United States has a more direct effect on habitat integrity than the white-tailed deer."

Hunting Helps Control Deer Overpopulation

Allen Pursell, Troy Weldy, and Mark White

In the following viewpoint, Allen Pursell, Troy Weldy, and Mark White argue that it is the forests that are endangered, and this is largely due to the habits and the overpopulation of white-tailed deer. The authors state that deer are changing the composition and the structure of forests by overeating and eliminating certain species, introducing and spreading the growth of new exotic non-native species, and even affecting the populations of songbirds. They argue that deer are just as catastrophic to forests as climate change and list specific actions that must be taken to control their impact. Allen Pursell is director of forest conservation at The Nature Conservancy. Troy Weldy is director of ecological management at The Nature Conservancy. Mark White is former director of Maui programs at The Nature Conservancy.

"Too Many Deer: A Bigger Threat to Eastern Forests than Climate Change?" by Allen Pursell, Troy Weldy, Mark White, August 22, 2013. This story originally appeared on Cool Green Science, the blog of The Nature Conservancy.

As you read, consider the following questions:

1. What methods do the authors use to substantiate their statements about the effects of deer overpopulation on forests?
2. What feature of the text adds credibility to the authors' claims?
3. What are some of the actions being taken to reduce the impact of deer?

In August, 2012 The Bloomberg View published a staff editorial entitled "Deer Infestation Calls for Radical Free-Market Solution." *The Wall Street Journal* then ran a story in November 2012 entitled America Gone Wild, noting the impact of overabundant deer. If business news organizations can talk freely about deer, The Nature Conservancy (TNC) needs to speak openly as well. Aldo Leopold long ago warned us of the problems of a growing deer herd. Have we waited too long to heed his advice, or is there still time to reverse the damage done?

No native vertebrate species in the eastern United States has a more direct effect on habitat integrity than the white-tailed deer. There are no hard numbers, but in many states deer populations continue to rise well beyond historical norms. In many areas of the country deer have changed the composition and structure of forests by preferentially feeding on select plant species.

In northern Minnesota, TNC staff demonstrated that decades of overbrowsing led to recruitment failure for many tree species, a shift in subcanopy and canopy dominance towards non-preferred white spruce, and significantly lower forest productivity (White 2012). In New York, TNC scientists report that one-third of New York's forests are currently compromised as a result of excessive herbivory.

Findings similar to these have been documented across the country. US Forest Service researchers have noted that even if areas with high deer densities were managed to reduce the impact of deer, there may be long-lasting legacy effects (Royo 2010). Webster (2005) found severe and lasting impacts at Smoky Mountain National Park to be so complete that some plants such as trilliums were unlikely to recolonize local areas on their own. Deer are also well-documented vectors for the dispersal of non-native exotic plants (Knight et al. 2009, Baiser et al. 2008, Williams and Ward 2006).

Indirect effects on wildlife have been reported as well, such as widespread declines of North American songbird populations (Chollet 2012). One study found forest songbirds that preferred nesting in the shrub and intermediate canopy layer declined in abundance and species richness as deer density increased (deCalesta 1994).

White-tailed deer likely impact every landscape east of the Mississippi River. The damage has been insidious—both slow moving and cumulative. Unfortunately, the harm is often overlooked, or worse, accepted as somehow "natural."

In our opinion, no other threat to forested habitats is greater at this point in time—not lack of fire, not habitat conversion, not climate change. Only invasive exotic insects and disease have been comparable in magnitude. We can argue about which threat is more significant than another, but no one who walks the eastern forests today can deny the impact of deer to forest condition.

It is clearly true that fire suppression has had a widespread impact on successional trajectory and tree species composition. A natural fire return interval would be a great benefit to many eastern forests. Yet even where fire is present, excessive deer herbivory has been shown to depress tree species diversity or at least minimize the benefits of fire. In the words of a recent study on the interactions of fire, canopy gaps, and deer browsing: "… restoring disturbances without controlling browsing may be counterproductive." (Nuttle, 2013)

While we acknowledge that climate change is a long-term stressor that will lead to significant changes in eastern forest ecosystems, high deer populations have had a much greater negative impact currently and over the last several decades. At present there is little evidence of direct climate change impacts on eastern forests (Beckage et al. 2008, Woodall et al. 2009, Zhu et al. 2012, Rustad et al. 2012). With climate envelope and other modeling systems, we have a general understanding about likely range shifts and compositional changes in eastern forests over the next 50-100 years. However, due to the many interacting factors such as atmospheric deposition (nitrogen, ozone), insect pests and pathogens, invasive plants, CO_2 enrichment, longer growing seasons, and white-tailed deer populations, there is a high degree of uncertainty about the future condition and function of eastern forests in a changing climate (Frelich and Reich 2009, Rustad et al. 2013).

No such uncertainty exists regarding the negative impacts of high deer populations on eastern forests; the body of evidence is unequivocal. In this article, we present only a small fraction of the literature on deer impacts. Reducing the impact of deer herbivory is currently a key forest restoration strategy (White 2012, Nuttle et al. 2013) and likely will become more important in order to help maintain resilient, functioning forests in a warming climate (Galatowitsch et al.2009).

Engaging society to address the problem will be difficult, probably similar to our experience with wild pig eradication in California and Hawaii, but on a wider scale. Views on deer management are deeply entrenched, both among those who hunt and those who don't. People have strong opinions when it comes to deer.

A Call to Action

Change is possible but it won't be easy or quick.

Deer management cannot be regulated at the federal level. As early as 1896 the Supreme Court ruled that states have "ownership" of their wildlife. As a result, each state has its own intricate rules. State regulations need not be standardized, but efforts at reform must be made state-by-state. This process will be slow as rules are generally promulgated by processes that ensure adequate evaluation by respective wildlife authorities and to allow for public review.

Nevertheless, some states are beginning to do the difficult work of changing policies to stabilize or reduce the number of deer. For example, Indiana recently enacted the first modern firearms season targeting female deer in the state's history.

It will be difficult to overcome traditional hunter concepts of proper deer management as it is counter-intuitive to most hunters that fewer game animals are desirable. Decades of effort, patience, and expense were invested to enhance populations to the point where hunting success is now commonplace. To suggest that populations be reduced and therefore increase the effort needed to harvest a deer understandably generates resistance. Success will take a carefully crafted and sustained public relations effort.

Like almost all conservation problems, deer management is a societal issue. If the deer population is to be reduced, it must be reduced slowly. Rules that lower the population drastically will almost certainly spur a backlash from hunters who can appeal to their respective legislatures to overturn regulations they regard as harsh. In an effort to lower the population of deer in Wisconsin the DNR liberalized hunting dramatically.

The result was a hunter revolt. Gov. Scott Walker campaigned on a pledge to fix deer management. Once elected, he made good on that promise by appointing a deer trustee to evaluate his state's DNR. The trustee's final report noted that by failing to adequately communicate with hunters and involve them in determining solutions the DNR had lost credibility (Kroll 2012). A similar push back may be occurring in Pennsylvania.

In some sense one of the greatest losses of all is that deer are no longer viewed as the majestic and even mystical animals of the forest that they were only a few decades ago. To quote Bloomberg: "… it's hard to think of a more insidious threat to forests, farms and wildlife, not to mention human health and safety, than deer."

How different that is from the time of John Muir, who wrote, "Standing, lying down, walking, feeding, running even for its life, it [deer] is always invincibly graceful, and adds beauty and animation to every landscape—a charming animal and a great credit to nature."

References

Allan B.F., L.S. Goessling, G.A. Storch, and R.E. Thach. 2010. Blood meal analysis to identify reservoir hosts for Amblyomma americanum ticks. Emerging Infectious Disease 16(3):433-440.

Baiser, B.J., L. Lockwood, D. La Puma, and M.F.J. Aronson. 2008. A perfect storm: two ecosystem engineers interact to degrade deciduous forests of New Jersey. Biological Invasions 10: 785-795.(Beckage, Osborne et al. 2008)

Beckage, B., B. Osborne, et al. 2008. A rapid upward shift of a forest ecotone during 40 years of warming in the Green Mountains of Vermont. Proc Natl Acad Sci USA 105: 4197-4202.

Beckage, B., B. Osborne, D.G. Gavin, C. Pucko, T. Siccama and T. Perkins 2008). "A rapid upward shift of a forest ecotone during 40 years of warming in the Green Mountains of Vermont." Proc Natl Acad Sci USA 105(11): 4197-4202.

Bloomberg View. (2012, August 8). Deer infestation calls for Radical Free-Market Solution. Bloomberg.com. Retrieved January 18, 2013 from http://www.bloomberg.com/.

Chollet, S. and J. Martin. 2012. Declining woodland birds in North America: should we blame Bambi? Diversity and Distributions doi: 10.1111/ddi.12003.

Conover, M.R. 1998. Perceptions of American agricultural producers about wildlife on their farms and ranches. Wildlife Society Bulletin 26(3):597-604.

deCalesta, D.S. 1994. Effect of white-tailed deer on songbirds within managed forests in Pennsylvania. Journal of Wildlife Management 58(4): 711-718.

Fagerstone, K.A. and W. H. Clay. 1997. Overview of USDA Animal Damage Control Efforts to Manage Overabundant Deer. Wildlife Society Bulletin 25(2): 413-417.

Frelich, L.E. and P.B. Reich. 2010. Will environmental changes reinforce the impact of global warming on the prairie–forest border of central North America? Frontiers in Ecology and the Environment 8: 371-378.

Galatowitsch, S., L. Frelich. 2009. Regional climate change adaptation strategies for biodiversity conservation in a midcontinental region of North America. Biological Conservation 142: 2012-2022.

Knight, T.M., J.L. Dunn, L.A. Smith, J. Davis, and S. Kalisz. 2009. Deer facilitate invasive plant success in Pennsylvania forest understory. Natural Areas Journal 29(2): 110-116.

Kroll, J.C., D.C. Guynn, Jr, and G.L. Alt. 2012. Final Report and Recommendations by Wisconsin White-tailed Deer Trustee and Review Committee. 2012. Madison, Wisconsin. 136 pp.

Nuttle, T., A.A. Royo, M.B. Adams, and W.P. Carson. 2013. Historic disturbance regimes promote tree diversity only under low browsing regimes in eastern deciduous forest. Ecological Monographs 83(1): 3-17.

Royo, A.A., S.L. Stout, D.S. deCalesta, T.G. Pierson. 2010. Restoring forest herb communities through landscape-level deer herd reductions: Is recovery limited by legacy effects? Biological Conservation 143: 2425-2434.

Rustad, L., J. Campbell, J. Dukes, T. Huntington, K. Fallon Lambert, J. Mohan, N. Rodenhouse. 2012. Changing Climate, Changing Forests: The Impacts of Climate

Change on Forests of the Northeastern United States and Eastern Canada. USDA Forest Service, Northern Research Station General Technical Report NRS-99: 56pp.

State Farm Mutual Automobile Insurance Co. (2012, October 23). It's West Virginia Again. Mountain State Leads State Farm's List of States Where Deer-Vehicle Confrontations Are Most Likely. Statefarm.com. Retrieved January 18, 2013 from http://www.statefarm.com/.

Wall Street Journal. (2012, November 2). America Gone Wild. online.wsj.online.com. Retrieved January 18, 2013 from http://online.wsj.com/.

Webster, C.R., M.A. Jenkins, J.H. Rock. 2005. Long-term response of spring flora to chronic herbivory and deer exclusion in Great Smoky Mountains National Park, USA. Biological Conservation 125: 297–307.

White, M.A. 2012. Long-term effects of deer browsing: Composition, structure, and productivity in a northeastern Minnesota old-growth forest. Forest Ecology and Management 269:222-228.

Williams, S.C. and J.S. Ward. 2006. Exotic seed dispersal by white-tailed deer in southern Connecticut. Natural Areas Journal 26(4): 383-390.

Woodall, C.W., C.M. Oswalt, J.A. Westfall, C.H. Perry, and A.O. Finley. 2009. An indicator of tree migration in the eastern United States. Forest Ecology and Management 257: 1434-1444.

Zhu, K., C.W. Woodall and J.S. Clark. 2012. Failure to migrate: lack of tree range expansion in response to climate change. Global Change Biology 18: 1042-1052.

> "*The non-lethal 'fear effects' from carnivores can constrain prey populations as strongly as—if not stronger than—actual kills made by carnivores.*"

"Fear Effects" Can Manage Populations More Effectively Than Lethal Strategies

Jennie Miller

In the following viewpoint, Jennie Miller explores the idea that populations of animals such as deer, which are creating damage and spreading illness through overpopulation, may react to humans taking over the role of the absent predators that once kept deer numbers under control. She states that the methods currently being used to control deer populations, such as culling and limiting births, are not effective, and that hunting or other non-lethal methods of instilling fear and distrust in the deer population can eventually work better. Jennie Miller is senior scientist at the Center for Conservation Innovation at Defenders of Wildlife in Washington, D.C.

"Hunting with Fear: Can Humans Fill the Role of Large Carnivores?" by Jennie Miller, Yale School of Forestry & Environmental Studies, June 13, 2014. Reprinted by permission.

As you read, consider the following questions:

1. How does the "fear effect" of predators work on prey animals?
2. What does the author mean by "hunting for fear"?
3. What area some of the negative effects that could result from an increasing presence of humans in wild areas?

In suburban neighborhoods across the globe, it is no longer surprising to see deer grazing outside downtown offices in the mid-day sun, brazenly snacking along sidewalks or grazing on gardens as pedestrians pass within petting distance. These animals, once cherished for their shy and flighty nature, now boldly roam among humans and their property, spreading disease and environmental devastation in their wake. Managers have had little success in their attempts to control overabundant ungulates with common methods such as culling and contraceptives, which are also costly and controversial. However, a recent review published in the *Journal of Applied Ecology* presents a new wildlife management tool that may offer a less bloody and more effective alternative: fear.

Over the past decade, ecologists have found mounting evidence of an idea that horror films have exploited over the last century—that the threat of death is scarier than death itself. Just as countless starlets have cowered from mere threats of torture from dark-hooded movie murders, prey animals make great sacrifices to avoid the simple threat of attack from wild carnivores. Just the presence of predators—be they tarantulas, terns or tigers—can elevate stress levels in their prey that hamper feeding, reproduction and ultimately survival. In essence, predators terrify their prey long before they pounce.

The non-lethal "fear effects" from carnivores can constrain prey populations as strongly as—if not stronger than—actual kills made by carnivores. Yet most management programs aimed at reducing overabundant deer populations have ignored fear effects, instead using methods such as hunting and birth control that rely on

What Are Endangered and Threatened Species?

A century ago, a bird called the passenger pigeon lived in North America. There were so many passenger pigeons that people often saw great flocks of them flying overhead containing thousands, even millions, of birds. Today, there is not a single one left. What happened?

The passenger pigeon became extinct. All living passenger pigeons disappeared from the earth entirely. The passenger pigeon became extinct for two reasons. First, the forests where it lived were cut down to make way for farms and cities. Second, many pigeons were shot for sport and because they were good to eat. At that time, there were no hunting laws to protect endangered species like there are now.

There are over 1,300 endangered or threatened species in the United States today. Endangered species are those plants and animals that have become so rare they are in danger of becoming extinct. Threatened species are plants and animals that are likely to become endangered within the foreseeable future throughout all or a significant portion of its range.

mortality alone to control ungulates. In their March 2013 article, Dr. Joris Cromsig and colleagues highlight the importance of incorporating fear effects into ungulate management. Humans should, basically, scare ungulates to death.

Cromsig et al. suggest adapting current practices of hunting to generate greater fear in ungulates. By extending the hunting season and area, hunters could evoke greater and more constant levels of fear in ungulates, creating stress that reduces herd sizes and shifts grazing patterns. But can humans adequately fill the role of large carnivores and limit ungulate populations through fear alone? As a doctoral student who spends hours contemplating how fear affects prey, I found Cromsig et al.'s suggestion intriguing yet in need of additional discussion.

Species disappear because of changes to the earth that are caused either by nature or by the actions of people. Sometimes a natural event, like a volcano erupting, can kill an entire species. Other times, extinction will happen slowly as nature changes our world.

People can also cause the extinction of plants and animals. The main reason that many species are endangered or threatened today is because people have changed the homes or habitats upon which these species depend. A habitat includes not only the other plants and animals in an area, but all of the things needed for the species' survival—from sunlight and wind to food and shelter. Pollution can also affect wildlife and contribute to extinction. The Nashville crayfish is endangered mainly because the creek where it lives has been polluted by people. Pesticides and other chemicals can poison plants and animals if they are not used correctly.

People can also endanger plants and animals by moving, or introducing, new species into areas where they do not naturally live. Some of these species do so well in their new habitat that they endanger those species already living there, called the native species. These introduced species are called invasive species.

"Learn More About Threatened and Endangered Species," United States Environmental Protection Agency.

In applying ideas about the "ecology of fear" to practical management, Cromsig and colleagues contribute to an emerging conversation on predation risk as a management tool (for examples see Berger 2007 and Treves et al. 2011). Non-lethal fear effects do appear to have great—and largely unexplored—utility for wildlife management issues such as ungulate overgrazing, livestock depredation and carnivore conservation. And by infusing fear effects into current practices of hunting implemented in countries worldwide, Cromsig et al. present a technique that could generate drastic changes with minimal cost and effort.

While the theoretical framework is strong, several limitations offer challenges in implementing the idea of "hunting for fear" as a management tool. For one, ecologists have yet to fully understand how the fear of carnivores varies spatially and temporally, as well as with predator hunting mode, so simulating fear effects in nature would be difficult. Furthermore, because game management involves humans as much as animals, hunters would need to adapt their fear effects uniquely by location to meet both cultural expectations and ecosystem composition. Cromsig and colleagues recognize these challenges and discuss them in their article.

However, several additional issues would be valuable to consider when deciding whether and how to implement "hunting for fear" for ungulate control. First, increasing human activity in natural spaces—even as a management tool—must be scrupulously considered because these efforts could easily result in unintended side effects on the ecosystem. Recreating carnivore fear effects with humans would be most applicable in areas where carnivore populations have been extirpated or reduced to densities where predators no longer generate significant fear effects on prey populations. If predators are still present in the environment (and even if they are not), the presence of humans could strongly disturb the ecosystem, creating more problems than solutions. Most carnivores, as well as numerous other species, are highly sensitive to human presence and spatially and/or temporally avoid human activity, altering their behaviors and roles within the food web. These types of unintended side effects on the ecosystem must be examined carefully prior to implementation to determine whether 'hunting for fear' could do more harm than good.

Second, even with a low predator density, encouraging humans to spend more time in wild spaces might inflate human-wildlife conflict in parts of the world. For instance, bringing humans into jungles with low densities of tigers and leopards in an attempt to control their populous prey species (such as wild pigs and nilgai antelope, which are considered some of the worst crop-raiding pests in southeast Asia) could displace big cats from their last remaining habitats, cause them to hunt livestock and/or encourage attacks on people. At the least, increasing the chance of confrontation between humans and large carnivores could likely further amplify negative attitudes towards carnivores that already create challenges for conservation. Thus, "hunting for fear" should likely not be attempted in locations where dangerous large carnivores still exist, even in low densities.

Considering these concerns, it appears that 'hunting for fear' might generate the greatest ecological benefits with the fewest negative repercussions on humans and wild species alike in areas where carnivores have been extirpated and ungulate control is desperately needed to restore ecosystem health. Prime examples include the urban areas of many developed countries in Europe and North America, such as the United States where Cromsig et al. point to over-browsing by white-tailed deer (Odocoileus virginianus) as the cause of the extinction of species such as White trillium (*Trillium grandiflorum*). In these areas where large carnivores are locally extinct, people could functionally replace the fear effects on prey that carnivores once created when food webs were intact. Indeed, this possibility speaks to the powerful role that humans can play in the ecosystem and illustrates the importance of a new perspective that incorporates humans into food webs, such as human-nature coupling (Liu et al. 2007).

The incorporation of fear into hunting as a management tool requires careful forethought and small-scale experimentation to avoid devastating side effects, such as those that have accompanied the introduction of invasive species to control agricultural pests. I encourage particular forethought prior to the application of "hunting for fear" in countries with poor forest management infrastructure, where hunting may be especially difficult to regulate.

Overall, incorporating fear effects into hunting may offer an innovative technique for controlling ungulate populations. "Hunting for fear" is a prime example of a practical tool that applies principles from species interactions to solve an ecological problem. These types of tools are rare yet essential if science-informed management is to rigorously address the complexities of species and ecosystem conservation.

> "*Today, more and more animal and plant species are on the verge of extinction because of a variety of major factors that cause a species to become endangered, and as you might expect, humans play a role in quite a few of them.*"

Human Encroachment Is the Biggest Threat to Animal Endangerment

Jennifer Bove

In the following viewpoint, Jennifer Bove presents very specific factors why certain animals are either extinct or close to extinct. In addition to reasons that are familiar to many people, such as illegal hunting and habitat loss and destruction, the author also explores the introduction of non-native or invasive species to habitats. Jennifer Bove is a wildlife expert and a contributing writer for the National Wildlife Foundation. She is the author of a series of children's nonfiction books about animals, published by HarperCollins.

"Reasons Animals Become Endangered," by Jennifer Bove, Dotdash publishing family, July 7, 2019. Reprinted by permission.

As you read, consider the following questions:

1. Is the author optimistic about efforts to save endangered animals?
2. How do economics contribute to the likelihood of an animal becoming extinct?
3. What are some of the reasons for extinction that are not caused by humans?

When an animal species is considered endangered, it means that the International Union for Conservation of Nature (IUCN) has evaluated it as nearly extinct, which means that a significant portion of its range has already died off and the rate of birth is lower than the species' death rate.

Today, more and more animal and plant species are on the verge of extinction because of a variety of major factors that cause a species to become endangered, and as you might expect, humans play a role in quite a few of them. In fact, the biggest threat to endangered animals is human encroachment on their habitats.

Fortunately, conservation efforts around the world are bent on helping these endangered animals revitalize their dwindling populations through a variety of humanitarian efforts, including curtailing illegal poaching, halting pollution, and habitat destruction, and curtailing the introduction of exotic species into new habitats.

Habitat Destruction and Pollution

Every living organism needs a place to live, but a habitat is not just a residence, it is also where an animal finds food, raises its young and allows the next generation to take over. Unfortunately, humans destroy animal habitats in a number of different ways: building houses, clearing forests to get lumber and plant crops, draining rivers to bring water to those crops, and paving over meadows to make streets and parking lots.

In addition to physical encroachment, human development of animals' habitats pollutes the natural landscape with petroleum products, pesticides, and other chemicals, which destroys food sources and viable shelters for the creatures and plants of that area.

As a result, some species die outright while others are pushed into areas where they can't find food and shelter. Worse yet, when one animal population suffers it affects many other species in its food web so more than one species' population is likely to decline.

Habitat destruction is the number one reason for animal endangerment, which is why conservation groups work diligently to reverse the effects of human developments. Many non-profit groups like the Nature Conservancy clean up coastlines and establish nature preserves to prevent further harm to native environments and species around the world.

Introduction of Exotic Species Destroys Delicate Food Systems

An exotic species is an animal, plant, or insect that is introduced into a place where it did not evolve naturally. Exotic species often have a predatory or competitive advantage over native species, which have been a part of a particular biological environment for centuries, because even though native species are well adapted to their surroundings, they may not be able to deal with species that closely compete with them for food. Basically, native species haven't developed natural defenses for an exotic species and vice versa.

One example of endangerment due to both competition and predation is the Galapagos tortoise. Non-native goats were introduced to the Galapagos Islands during the 20th century. These goats fed on the tortoises' food supply, causing the number of tortoises to decline rapidly. Because the tortoises could not defend themselves or stop the overpopulation of goats on the island, they were forced to abandon their native feeding grounds.

Many countries have passed laws banning specific exotic species known to endanger native habitats from entering the country. Exotic species are sometimes referred to as invasive species, especially in cases of banning them. For instance, the United Kingdom has placed raccoons, mongooses, and cabbages on their invasive species list, all of which are barred from entering the country.

Illegal Hunting Can Endanger Species

When hunters ignore rules that regulate the number of animals that should be hunted (a practice known as poaching), they can reduce populations to the point that species become endangered. Unfortunately, poachers are often hard to catch because they are deliberately trying to evade authorities, and they operate in areas where enforcement is weak.

Furthermore, poachers have developed sophisticated techniques for smuggling animals. Baby bears, leopards, and monkeys have been sedated and stuffed into suitcases for transport. Live animals have been sold to people who want exotic pets or medical research subjects. And, animal pelts and other body parts are also secretly smuggled across borders and sold through black market networks of buyers who pay high prices for illegal animal products.

Even legal hunting, fishing, and gathering of wild species can lead to population reductions that cause species to become endangered. A lack of restriction on the whaling industry in the 20th century is one example. It wasn't until several whale species were nearing extinction that countries agreed to abide by an international moratorium. Some whale species have rebounded thanks to this moratorium but others remain at risk.

International laws forbid these practices, and there are a number of government and nongovernment organizations (NGOs) whose sole purpose is to stop illegal poaching, especially of animals like elephants and rhinoceroses. Thanks to the efforts of groups like the International Anti-Poaching Foundation and local conservation groups like the PAMS Foundation in Tanzania, these endangered species have human advocates fighting to protect them from outright extinction.

How Are Animals Endangered?

Of course, species endangerment and extinction can happen without human interference. Extinction is a natural part of evolution. Fossil records show that long before people came along, factors such as overpopulation, competition, sudden climatic change, and catastrophic events like volcanic eruptions and earthquakes drove the decline of numerous species.

There are a few warning signs that a species could become extinct. If a species has some economic importance, such as the Atlantic salmon, it may be at risk. Surprisingly, large predators, who we might expect to have an advantage over other species, are often at risk as well. This list includes grizzly bears, bald eagles, and gray wolves.

A species whose gestational period is lengthy, or who have small numbers of offspring at each birth has the potential to become endangered more readily. The mountain gorilla and California condor are two examples. And species with weak genetic makeup, like manatees or giant pandas, have more risk of extinction with each generation.

> "Not all non-native species cause biological or economic harm, and only a fraction become established and have an effect that is considered harmful. But non-native species can also have desirable effects on an ecosystem."

Non-Native Species Have Potential for Conservation

Martin A. Schlaepfer, Dov F. Sax, and Julian D. Olden

In the following excerpted viewpoint, Martin A. Schlaepfer, Dov F. Sax, and Julian D. Olden explore the idea that non-native species may actually benefit habitats and should also be preserved if they do not cause environmental or biological harm. They may even supply shelter and food for native species, may contribute to habitat restoration, and can substitute for native plants and animals that are no longer present in the ecosystem. Martin A. Schlaepfer is a conservation biologist and senior lecturer at the University of Geneva. Dov F. Sax is professor of ecology and evolutionary biology at Brown University. Julian D. Olden is an ecologist and professor in the School of Aquatic and Fishery Sciences at the University of Washington.

"The Potential Conservation Value of Non-Native Species," by Martin A. Schlaepfer, Dov F. Sax and Julian D. Olden, Society for Conservation Biology, November 3, 2010. Reprinted by permission.

As you read, consider the following questions:

1. How have scientists and society in general viewed non-native species in the past?
2. Name one specific way in which a non-native species can benefit a native habitat.
3. How might non-native species help to revive a habitat that is no longer able to support its native species?

Non-native species present a range of threats to native ecosystems and human well-being. Non-native predators and herbivores can cause extinctions of native species, particularly on islands and in freshwater ecosystems (Wilcove et al. 1998; Mooney & Hobbs 2000; Sax & Gaines 2008). Furthermore, they can alter the functioning of ecosystems and can carry infectious diseases that can endanger native species and human health (Vitousek et al. 1996; Daszak et al. 2000; Ehrenfeld 2003). By damaging commercial crops and interfering with industrial activities, non-native species are responsible for annual economic losses on the order of billions of US dollars per year (Pimentel et al. 2005). As a result governmental agencies and nongovernmental organizations are frequently mandated or have chosen to prevent the introduction of non-native species and minimize their negative effects (Millennium Ecosystem Assessment 2005; Lodge et al. 2006).

Not all non-native species cause biological or economic harm, and only a fraction become established and have an effect that is considered harmful (Williamson & Fitter 1996; Davis 2009). But non-native species can also have desirable effects on an ecosystem. For example, numerous species have been repeatedly and deliberately introduced outside their native range for agricultural, ornamental, and recreational purposes (Ewel et al. 1999). As a result non-native species are integral to the culture and economies of most countries. There have also been numerous recent examples of non-native species contributing to achievement of conservation objectives (e.g., Westman 1990; D'Antonio & Meyerson 2002; Gozlan 2008).

Subjective Views of Non-Native Species

Scientific and societal perceptions of non-native species have likely impeded consideration of the potential beneficial effects of non-native species. Most scientists investigating the effects of non-native species try to conduct their work objectively; nevertheless, several authors have demonstrated that a bias persists against non-native species among scientists (Slobodkin 2001; Gurevitch & Padilla 2004; Stromberg et al. 2009). These biases are reflected in the assumptions commonly made about the intrinsic and instrumental values of non-native species, the language used when describing them, and in the types of studies conducted (Sagoff 2005). For example, in a landmark study in which the response of biological diversity (encompassing genetic, species, and ecosystem diversity) to several natural and anthropogenic drivers were predicted, Sala et al. (2000) considered non-native species only as potential threats, not as contributors to a region's species richness. Furthermore, in studies in which an index of biotic integrity was used, the presence of non-native species decreases the index value even if the non-native species have no or little detectable biological effect (Parker et al. 1999). Finally, the language used to describe non-native species in the scientific literature is frequently scattered with militarized and xenophobic expressions (e.g., "war on aliens" and "American ecosystems under siege by alien invaders") (e.g., Peretti 1998; Krajick 2005; Larson 2005).

The consequences of these biases are difficult to quantify, but they almost certainly have resulted in an emphasis on documenting the negative economic and biological effects of non-native species (Pyšek et al. 2008). Studies that fail to find a negative effect (e.g., Nielsen et al. 2008) are likely underreported. Furthermore, numerous researchers have evaluated the economic costs associated with non-native species, and syntheses that estimate the total economic effect of non-native species (e.g., Pimentel et al. 2005; McIntosh et al. 2009) attract substantial attention. By contrast, relatively few researchers have quantified the economic benefits (e.g., value of pollination by non-native bees, fees paid to hunt non-native game) derived from non-native species (but see Southwick & Southwick 1992; Ackefors 1999; Pascual et al. 2009). As a result, there has not been a comprehensive review of the economic benefits provided by non-native species. The direct economic costs associated with wild and feral non-native species may well be greater than the income they generate, but we think both costs and income should be quantified.

We had two aims here. First, we sought to catalog the possible ways in which non-native species can help achieve conservation objectives. We did not review all the known negative effects of non-native species because these have been described exhaustively (e.g., Mooney & Hobbs 2000; Lodge et al. 2006). We also did not focus on economic or human-health effects. Instead, we considered examples of unplanned and intentional introductions of non-native species that contributed to achieving conservation objectives. We use the term non-native for species that occur outside of their historic range and invasive for cases in which these species cause biological, social, or economic harm.

Second, we investigated the role of non-native species in the broader context of setting conservation objectives. Traditionally, conservation goals have been defined by historical, static benchmarks aimed at protecting flagship species and "pristine" ecosystems and their putative integrity and stability (Forum 2004). But many non-native species are firmly established in their recipient ecosystems and cannot be eradicated; thus, novel approaches are required to manage them (Schlaepfer et al. 2005; Norton 2009). Furthermore, the negative and positive effects of non-native species vary over time, as will the manner in which these effects are perceived by humans, which in turn will have large effects on how non-native species are managed (Maris & Béchet 2010).

Current Uses of Non-Native Species to Conserve and Restore Species and Ecosystems

Many conservation efforts focus on the protection of genes, species, ecosystems, and their interactions. Numerous researchers have documented the various ways in which non-native species positively contribute to achieving conservation goals either serendipitously or intentionally. Conservation benefits include providing habitat, food, or trophic subsidies for native species, serving as catalysts for the restoration of native species, serving as substitutes for extinct ecosystem engineers, and providing ecosystem services.

Shelter and Food for Native Species

Non-native species can provide shelter (e.g., Wonham et al. 2005; Severns & Warren 2008) or be a nutritional resource (e.g., Bulleri et al. 2006; Carlsson et al. 2009) for native species. The potential role of non-native species in providing resources for rare native species is likely to be particularly important in situations when restoration of the native species that formerly provided shelter or an energy source is impractical due to limited economic resources or changes in the physical environment (e.g., Zavaleta et al. 2001; Hershner & Havens 2008). In the case of the non-native tamarisk (*Tamarix* spp.), preconceived notions appear to have contributed to an underestimation of its potential contributions to conservation. Tamarisk is a non-native woody plant that has become relatively common in riparian areas throughout the southwestern United States as a result of human activity and changes in hydrology (Stromberg et al. 2009). Initial reports suggested tamarisk were causing a drop in water table levels and reducing habitat quantity and quality for native riparian species, including the Southwestern Willow Flycatcher (*Empidonax traillii extimus*), which is listed as endangered under the US Endangered Species Act. As a result millions of US dollars were spent removing tamarisk with mechanical treatments, herbicides, and a herbivorous beetle (*Diorabda elongate*) (DeLoach et al. 2006). Nevertheless, results of recent field studies reveal that in some areas up to 75% of the

Southwestern Willow Flycatchers nest in tamarisk and that fledgling success associated with nests built in tamarisk was indistinguishable from success associated with nests built in native trees (Ellis et al. 2008; Sogge et al. 2008). In a recent review Stromberg et al. (2009) argue that many undesirable changes to water tables and displacement of native biota attributed to tamarisk are exaggerated or unfounded.

Given the substantial modification to flooding regimes by dams throughout the southwestern United States, it may be difficult in many areas to reestablish native taxa that formerly supported the Flycatcher. Thus, although removing tamarisk may provide a step toward restoring historic vegetation in these regions, doing so may unexpectedly cause direct harm to an endangered native species that now depends in part on tamarisk (Zavaleta et al. 2001; Shafroth et al. 2008). In locations with multiple non-native species, the control or eradication of one species will not necessarily result in the desired outcome because species interactions may be altered (Courchamp et al. 2003; Norton 2009; Chiba 2010).

Catalysts for Restoration

Non-native species that increase structural heterogeneity or complexity of an area are positively correlated with increases in abundance or species richness (Crooks 2002), and in some instances non-native species may therefore be useful catalysts for ecosystem restoration (Ewel & Putz 2004). For example, former pastures with sparse vegetation and eroded soils in Puerto Rico (USA) are not readily recolonized by native trees. By contrast, non-native plantation trees are able to survive and subsequently attract seed dispersers and establish microclimates in which native plants can reestablish (Lugo 1997; Rodriguez 2006). In one study, 20 native woody species recolonized deforested land 8 years after non-native trees were planted, whereas only one native woody species colonized unplanted control plots (Parrotta 1999).

Substitutes for Extinct Taxa

Non-native species are sometimes deliberately introduced to fill an ecological niche formerly occupied by a closely related species (Donlan et al. 2006; Griffiths et al. 2010). Non-native species do not have the same cultural and historical value as native species, but they have been used as acceptable ecological substitutes in cases where the benefits of their ecological function are perceived to exceed the potential risks of introducing a non-native species. For example, Aldabra giant tortoises (*Aldabrachelys gigantea*) have been introduced to several small islands surrounding Mauritius, where they appear to have successfully substituted the herbivory and seed-dispersal functions of native tortoises that recently became extinct (Griffiths et al. 2010).

In other cases the substitute roles provided by nonnative species have been more serendipitous. For example, in Hawaii (USA), non-native species of birds are now the primary dispersers of seeds and fruits of some native plant species with native dispersers that have become extinct or been extirpated from lowland vegetation (Foster & Robinson 2007). Non-native birds may have contributed to the extinction of several native bird species (by serving as vectors of avian malaria to which native bird species are susceptible (Kilpatrick 2006), but the remaining native species of plants and current ecosystems may now depend on the ecological roles of such substitute species.

[...]

Ecological Roles in Rapidly Changing Ecosystems

Non-native species could come to fill important ecosystem and aesthetic functions, particularly in places where native species cannot persist due to environmental changes. Indeed, some non-native species may be preadapted or adapt rapidly to the novel ecological conditions (Byers 2002). Furthermore, the ability of non-native species to tolerate and adapt to a broad range of biotic and abiotic conditions, as well as to expand their ranges rapidly, suggests they may persist under a variety of future climate scenarios (Dukes & Mooney 1999; Muth & Pigliucci 2007; Williams & Jackson 2007).

Non-native species contribute to local species richness (Sax & Gaines 2008) and thus may also contribute to ecosystem resilience and stability. Research has focused on species interactions (e.g., predation, herbivory) that can lead to declines in abundance of native species. Nevertheless, much less attention has been given to how food webs may be altered by the presence of non-native species (although see Byrnes et al. 2007) and whether long periods of time are necessary for strong positive links to form among species. Certainly, ecosystems that are composed mostly of non-native species can have complex species interactions and community structure (Wilkinson 2004). Therefore, it seems likely that nonnative species will often contribute to some of the putative benefits of species-rich ecosystems, such as increased productivity and stability (Hooper et al. 2005; Cardinale et al. 2007), but this proposition has not been tested.

[...]

Periodical and Internet Sources Bibliography

The following articles have been selected to supplement the diverse views presented in this chapter.

Evan Andrews, "Were Humans Responsible for Killing Off the Wooly Mammoth?" History.com, August 29, 2018. https://www.history.com/news/were-humans-responsible-for-killing-off-the-wooly-mammoth

Conserve Energy Future, "What Is Overhunting?" Accessed December 27, 2019. https://www.conserve-energy-future.com/causes-effects-solutions-overhunting.php

Alex Czartoryski, "10 Animals Hunted (or Nearly Hunted) to Extinction." Fresh Air Educators, September 28, 2011. https://www.huntercourse.com/blog/2011/08/10-animals-hunted-or-nearly-hunted-to-extinction

Javier C. Hernández, "China Reverses Ban on Rhino and Tiger Parts in Medicine, Worrying Activists." *New York Times*, October 29, 2018. https://www.nytimes.com/2018/10/29/world/asia/china-rhino-tiger-poaching.html

Karen Kirkpatrick, "Have Invasive Species Caused Any Extinctions?" How Stuff Works. https://science.howstuffworks.com/environmental/green-science/have-invasive-species-caused-extinctions.htm

Last Chance for Animals.org. "Hunting." https://www.lcanimal.org/index.php/campaigns/animals-in-entertainment/hunting

Frank Miniter, "Embracing 9 of the Non-Native and Invasive Species That We Love to Hunt and Fish." *Outdoor Life*, February 22, 2016. https://www.outdoorlife.com/articles/hunting/2016/02/embracing-9-non-native-and-invasive-species-we-love-hunt-and-fish

Olivia Rosane, "Invasive Species Have Led to a Third of Animal Extinctions Since 1500." Ecowatch, March 4, 2019. https://www.ecowatch.com/invasive-species-animal-extinctions-2630614032.html

Michael Schwartz, "Culling to Conserve: A Hard Truth for Lion Conservation." *National Geographic*, February 25, 2016. https://

blog.nationalgeographic.org/2016/02/25/culling-to-conserve-a
-hard-truth-for-lion-conservation

Science Daily, "Trophy Hunting May Cause Extinction in a Changing
Environment." November 28, 2017. https://www.sciencedaily
.com/releases/2017/11/171128230410.htm

Meilan Solly, "Human Hunting Is Driving the World's Biggest
Animals Toward Extinction." *Smithsonian Magazine*, February 7,
2019. https://www.smithsonianmag.com/smart-news
/human-hunting-worlds-biggest-animals-megafauna
-extinction-180971437

United States Environmental Protection Agency, "Summary of the
Endangered Species Act." https://www.epa.gov/laws-regulations
/summary-endangered-species-act

Mindy Weisberger, "Hunting Big Game: Why People Kill Animals
for Fun." *Scientific American*, May 28, 2017. https://www
.scientificamerican.com/article/hunting-big-game-why-people
-kill-animals-for-fun

Isabelle Catherine Winder, "Climate Change Is Putting Even Resilient
and Adaptable Animals Like Baboons at Risk." The Conversation,
May 16, 2019. https://theconversation.com/climate-change-is
-putting-even-resilient-and-adaptable-animals-like-baboons-at
-risk-115588

Justin Worland, "Research Shows Just How Much Hunting Reduces
Animal Populations." *Time*, April 13, 2017. https://time
.com/4736526/hunting-reduces-animal-populations

CHAPTER 4

Do Hunting Laws Contribute to Food Chain Imbalance?

Chapter Preface

Animals do not exist in a vacuum. In some way, and to some larger or smaller extent, every animal relies on some other animal or plant for survival. It might be an animal eating a certain species of plant to survive, a predator killing and eating a smaller prey animal, or even an insect that pollinates a flower and allows a plant species to grow and flourish. These types of interactions within a habitat are called food chains or food webs, and they are an interconnected group of plants and animals that all rely on other members of that web or on that chain in order to survive. Food webs and chains are basically an exchange of energy from one species to another, and they are the means by which the environment is balanced.

However, these food relationships can be disrupted by many different factors, such as a change in habitat because of climate change or overdevelopment, the loss of a predator or prey animal that allows a species to become overpopulated, and by the hunting or trapping of certain animals by humans. Another argument that frequently occurs between hunters and non-hunters is whether hunting in itself contributes to a food chain imbalance by damaging the percentage of predator and prey animals in a specific place. Hunters feel that they actually can help keep the food chain intact by helping to reduce the populations of animals that have become too great in number. They also feel that hunting laws and regulations prevent the overhunting of important predator species, and that the money spent on hunting licenses and other fees pays for the conservation of habitats and species.

As with many environmental issues, there are credible arguments on both sides of the question about food chains and the effects that hunters have on them. The food web issue is a delicate one, however, and will become increasingly important as climate change also begins to put stress on food webs and the different animals and plants that inhabit them.

> *"As human population continues to grow, and resources become limited, conservation successes may become harder to come by, scientists say."*

Managing Natural Resources Is Complex

Shreya Dasgupta

In the following viewpoint, Shreya Dasgupta looks at conservation and focuses on people as being the part of the food chain that is out of balance due to overpopulation and the shrinking of natural resources. Conservation efforts that attempt to keep the human-animal relationship balanced have often failed, due to several specific factors, not the least of which is poaching and illegal hunting. Poor environmental decisions and lack of law enforcement are impeding attempts to rebalance food webs. Shreya Dasgupta is a science and environmental writer based in India. A former wildlife researcher, her work has appeared in BBC Earth, New Scientist, *Ensia, the Scientist, and the* Guardian.

"5 Reasons Why Many Conservation Efforts Fail," by Shreya Dasgupta, Mongabay.com, March 30, 2016. Reprinted by permission.

As you read, consider the following questions:

1. What effects is the increasing human population having on animals and habitats?
2. What is one of the reasons why conservation efforts are not successful, according to the viewpoint?
3. Why are local communities important in the conservation effort?

One aim of conservation projects is to protect wild habitats and prevent species extinction. But managing natural resources is complex. Despite striving for years, conservation groups—both big and small—often struggle to find that perfect recipe for success.

Some conservation efforts have seen triumph. For example, the recovery of the southern white rhinoceros (*Ceratotherium simum ssp. simum*) is considered to be one of the biggest conservation success stories in recent times.

In the 1800s, the southern white rhino was considered extinct. But thanks to intensive efforts that involved creation of protected areas and captive breeding of the rhinos, this sub-species went from a tiny, single population of less than 50 individuals in 1895 to more than 20,000 individuals. Now, the southern white rhino is the most abundant of all the rhinos.

Often though, such wins are short-lived. In the case of the southern white rhino, for example, a recent uptick in rampant poaching carried out by organized criminal networks is seriously threatening the rhino's survival and undermining conservationists' efforts.

As human population continues to grow, and resources become limited, conservation successes may become harder to come by, scientists say.

"To be blunt, we are feeding and breeding like hungry migratory locusts," William Laurance, a Distinguished Research Professor at James Cook University, told Mongabay. "When my grandfather was a boy, we had a billion people on Earth; today we have well over seven billion, and we could well be heading toward ten billion or more. To this point in time, we've survived by continually exploiting new frontiers—for minerals, timber, oil, and other goods—but we're running out of new frontiers to exploit."

And this can spell trouble for wildlife and wild lands. In fact, despite efforts to curb species extinction, "the average risk of extinction for birds, mammals, amphibians and corals show no sign of decreasing," according to the United Nation's Global Biodiversity Outlook 4 report.

Lack of Local Buy-In

Every year, new protected areas are chalked out across the world. Often, these are created in developing countries, which are both rich in biodiversity and have some of the poorest populations in the world.

Traditionally though, protected areas have been designed to exclude local communities. In some cases, such as in parks that have sufficient manpower and resources to physically patrol and guard the parks effectively, or when local communities have voluntarily moved out of the parks after being adequately consulted and compensated, this "preservation" conservation strategy has worked.

But as people and wildlife scramble for space, excluding local people from conservation efforts in increasingly becoming a recipe for failure in the long run.

According to a 2013 review study, displacing local communities from their traditional lands, restricting their access to resources within the parks, and providing little or no compensation, can make them hostile towards the conservation groups and their efforts. Often, this leads to conflict, compelling the communities to go against the established rules, and harvest resources and hunt illegally.

"If the local people do not see a benefit of local conservation, then whatever the laws are, they are going to be ineffective," Stuart Pimm, a Professor of conservation ecology at the Duke University, told Mongabay.

Failing to consider the people who live in and around protected areas can have disastrous consequences. It can delay projects, cause conservationists and governments to miss their conservation targets, and cost billions of dollars because of the ensuing conflict.

However, like all conservation strategies, community-based conservation must be carefully designed, scientists say.

"Truth be said, a lot of local management does not work very well," Laurance said. "That's not to imply that top-down management of parks and other lands is perfect either. I actually think that almost everything is context-dependent."

Ignoring History

One problem, according to some experts, is that conservationists tend to apply conservation strategies far too generally. They fail to understand the past and current ecology of the place, its wildlife, politics and people. And this can lead to failure.

Studies have shown, for instance, that conservation groups often fail to look into past patterns of human population densities in and around proposed protected areas. They also fail to delve into the history of land tenure, conflict and resource use in the forests or habitats they want to protect.

Conservation groups also tend to plan their projects based on a number of misleading assumptions, experts say. One such assumption, for instance, is that conservationists tend to look at local communities as socially homogenous groups of people. Project planners often fail to appreciate the complexities of gender, households, different institutes and individuals within communities, which can result in conflict and failure.

Planners also tend to assume that local people are destructive to biodiversity conservation. While this may be true in some cases, this blanket assumption means that conservation groups sometimes ignore the true dynamics of the local communities' agricultural and hunting practices, and how these are adapted to the local socio-ecological conditions.

"Unless you understand the local politics, you're not going to be successful," Pimm said. "Now, I'm never going to understand that completely. I don't live in those places. But I can do my best, and I can recognize that I have to work with the people and the local politics."

Lack of Funding

Biodiversity protection requires money. But conservation groups often struggle to find reliable sources of funding that can ensure long-term success of their conservation initiatives.

"A big problem is that we tend to have funding models based on three- to five-year cycles," Laurance said. "We start a project and then expect quick and, ideally, long-term results. But things fall apart once the funding stops. You can't throw dollars in the short term at complex problems and expect long-term success."

When funding does become available, it is often unevenly distributed or biased towards certain groups of animals. A study published in 2010, for example, found that "charismatic" species of mammals were more likely to find scientific funding than other "less attractive" reptiles, birds or amphibians. Similarly, a study published this month found that only 12 percent of endangered species on the US endangered species lists are receiving as much funding as prescribed in their recovery plan.

Sometimes though, availability of funds does not guarantee that biodiversity conservation efforts will be fruitful. According to Pimm, this is a problem with many large conservation groups. Large groups are more interested in raising large sums of money, he said, rather than spending them well.

"This is the reason why I founded SavingSpecies with some very distinguished conservation scientists," he added. "We felt that small conservation groups are first of all small, and that makes them vulnerable. Big conservation groups are sucking the funding out. So we wanted to do our best to empower and encourage all local groups simply because we believe that they are more effective at what they do than the bigger groups."

Lack of Clearly Stated Goals

All projects need goals. Conservation initiatives, too, start with goals and objectives that the groups want to achieve within a given period of time. These goals help chart out specific management actions as well as strategies to distribute money and resources that can make the conservation project a success.

Unfortunately, many conservation projects set out with very fuzzy, poorly designed goals, Pimm said. "These are usually set by people who are funding the projects rather than by the absolute priority of the conservation action that they are seeking," he added. "I think that sometimes the goals are not even very closely connected with conservation."

Conservation efforts benefit from straightforward goals and measurable objectives—both short-term and long-term—that are guided by the "best available" science. Such objectives can help evaluate the success of a conservation program.

Setting unrealistic or inconsistent goals, however, can seriously undermine conservation efforts. When local communities are involved, for example, changing objectives can lead to confusion among the community members regarding how the natural resources will be managed. This can in turn lead to frustration and failure of conservation efforts.

Conservation is complex, though. So defining clear objectives and quantitatively measuring the success of conservation efforts is not always possible or feasible.

"Let's say, for instance, that I teach a course in conservation practice, and one of my students happens to be the daughter of the director of national parks of a nation, and that she in turn inspires her father to establish series of new parks," Laurance said. "That's a very important outcome, but it's diffuse and indirect. How does one measure that sort of thing? Conservation success can happen in lots of ways that are not always easy to assess."

Lack of Law and Order

Poaching of rhinos and elephants is at an all time high. Yet, loopholes in existing laws, poor governance and lack of law enforcement are making it easy for poachers and traffickers to get away with their crimes.

Studies have shown that parks are more effective in protecting biodiversity when they have a higher density of guards patrolling them. Harsher punishments can also be deterrents to wildlife crimes. Often though, forest guards are insufficiently trained and equipped, and lack the means to patrol parks or fight against armed poachers.

Moreover, wildlife crimes such as poaching and illegal timber logging are increasingly becoming organized and are no longer limited to violations of national and international laws relating to the environment, according to a recent INTERPOL report. Wildlife crimes often intersect other offences such as murder, corruption, and the trafficking of drugs and weapons, making law enforcement by environment authorities particularly challenging, the report notes.

Tackling such complex crimes requires increased collaboration between various environmental and policing agencies, anti-money laundering networks and anti-corruption authorities.

"We need to push for cultural changes in which corruption and poor enforcement become less acceptable socially," Laurance said. "I'm not quite sure how to do this but a heck of a lot of bad environmental decisions are made because somebody is getting rich as a result."

> "Today in North America, not one
> threatened or endangered species
> is hunted, fished, or trapped
> and no species have become
> endangered because of modern,
> regulated hunting."

Controlled Hunting Is Environmentally Friendly

John Mills

In the following viewpoint, John Mills gives a brief overview of the history of hunting and humans, including times when there was a "dark past" hunting that led to species extinctions. However, the author argues that hunters are some of the biggest supporters of conservation and habitat preservation, and that controlled hunting can actually be beneficial to the environment. He feels that hunters and other groups working together are the best way to work toward environmental conservation.

"Controlled Hunting Is Environmentally Friendly," by John Mills, Province of Nova Scotia. Reprinted by permission.

As you read, consider the following questions:

1. What were some of the things that happened in the "dark past" of hunting?
2. What are the author's arguments for hunters being environmental advocates?
3. How does the author answer his own questions about whether humans really need to hunt?

Humans have always hunted. Food, clothing, tools, and shelter were mainly provided by harvesting wild plants and animals. Humans are animals, and like all species, are totally dependent on natural resources for survival. Humans are, have always been, and always will be a part of, and not apart from, nature. Whether, they choose to eat domesticated fruits and vegetables, processed foods, wild animals and plants, or farmed livestock, the environment (nature) is the source of all these foods.

Humans evolved as omnivores—creatures that eat both plant and animal materials. Like bears, raccoons, and painted turtles, humans are also predators. All predators have developed specialized physical features for hunting through time, such as talons, claws, or venom. Lacking such well-developed, natural adaptations, humans use their intelligence as an advantage when hunting. From hunting in groups using clubs and stones to the current use of modern firearms, humans have been successful at obtaining animal and plant foods from the wild.

But do humans really need to hunt? In today's technological society, there is fresh produce from California, frozen fish sticks, locally-grown greenhouse tomatoes, and many fast-food outlets. Aside from a few aboriginal cultures that still depend on hunting and gathering, who needs to hunt to survive?

In North America, many aboriginal people still hunt as part of their cultural and social traditions. Many non-natives also hunt as part of a chosen lifestyle that often includes activities, such as gardening, fishing, trapping, and cutting firewood. All these people hunt because they need and want to; it provides nutritious food for the table, allows one to provide for oneself, and fosters a closeness with the environment. But how does modern hunting impact on today's wildlife? Can humans kill wildlife and still expect healthy populations of animals to exist into the future?

All plant and animal species have evolved so that each has a strategy that helps to ensure their future survival. Many species produce more young than available habitat can support. There is only so much food and shelter available, particularly during the winter. These "surplus" animals die from a variety of causes—starvation, disease, predation, or accidents. Old age is seldom an option in the wild. Only those that elude predators, find enough food to sustain themselves, escape disease, and avoid accidents, will survive. Natural mortality factors help ensure that there is room for next year's crop of young. By being fruitful and multiplying, nature increases the chances that enough animals, young and adult, will survive to reproduce and perpetuate themselves next year.

Human predation on wildlife, through hunting, is strictly controlled by licence numbers, seasons, and bag limits. Part of the science of wildlife management is predicting safe harvest levels. Controlled hunting is not detrimental to animal populations. Modern wildlife management ensures that enough animals are left each year to replace those harvested by humans. When controlled hunting takes individual animals out of the population, they are replaced by others of their kind. Regulated hunting is an example of sustainable use of a renewable natural resource.

Hunting does have a dark past. Following the colonization of North America by Europeans, unregulated market hunting for hides, meat, feathers, and eggs was disastrous for wildlife species such as the passenger pigeon and the Labrador duck. By the mid-1800s, hunters and naturalists saw how destructive market hunting was. By the late 1800s and early 1900s, North America witnessed the first regulation of hunting. Hunters lobbied hard for these changes. Laws were established as to which species and sex could be taken. Length of hunting seasons and daily or seasonal quotas or bag limits were set. These early attempts at protection have been increased to the point today where there is a very complex arrangement of regulations designed to conserve wildlife resource. For today's wildlife agencies, conserving wildlife populations is the number one priority. Where numbers are sufficient, controlled hunting is allowed.

The single greatest threat to wildlife is habitat loss. Without habitat, there is no wildlife. Human encroachment, pollution, draining of wetlands, and development are taking land out of production for wildlife. When animals cease to exist because of habitat loss, they are gone—forever! Habitat destruction guarantees species disappearances and wildlife extinctions.

Through licence fees and donations, hunters have traditionally been the major contributors to programs aimed at saving and restoring wildlife habitat. Other groups have also been involved in protecting habitat. Hunters and non-hunters need to work together. Both groups want to achieve similar goals— abundant, diverse populations of wildlife existing in a healthy, pollution-free environment.

Collectively, hunting and non-hunting groups have restored and protected over 10,000 hectares of prime wetland habitat in Nova Scotia. Non-hunted and endangered species, as well as the traditional game animals, all benefit from habitat protection and restoration programs. Hunters and non-hunters should join forces to oppose land-use practises that are not environmentally or wildlife friendly, and to work together on solutions to these problems.

Hunting is not for everyone. However, in our modern, computer-age society, there are those who still choose to provide nutritious meat for their families, enjoy the natural experience of the chase, and desire to remain a part of the natural cycle of life and death. Hunting is a chosen lifestyle and one that is in harmony with the human role in nature. Hunting is not destructive to the natural world. Today in North America, not one threatened or endangered species is hunted, fished, or trapped and no species have become endangered because of modern, regulated hunting. Controlled hunting and gathering of wild foods are environmentally friendly. Too bad more human activities cannot legitimately make the same claim.

> *"Lions, wolves, pumas, lynxes and other major carnivores play key roles in keeping ecosystems in balance. The current depletion of numbers of major predators threatens to cause serious ecological problems across the globe."*

Threats to Lions, Leopards, and Wolves Endanger Us All

Robin McKie

In the following viewpoint, Robin McKie warns that large predators are vital to keeping ecosystems in balance and that there will be serious global problems if their numbers continue to be depleted. However, humans do not tolerate predator species well, especially when they affect livestock or agriculture, and in some parts of the world, large predators have also been overhunted or poached to the point where there are so few of them that their former prey animals are overpopulated. Robin McKie is science and environment editor for the Observer.

"How the Threat to Lions, Leopards and Wolves Endangers Us All," by Robin McKie, Guardian News and Media Limited, January 26, 2014. Reprinted by permission.

As you read, consider the following questions:

1. What happens to a food web when large predators are reduced in number?
2. How has species overpopulation affected African farmers specifically?
3. Give a specific example of how a change in the predator/ prey populations has affected other parts of a food web.

They are the planet's most prolific killers—and also some of nature's most effective protectors. This is the stark conclusion of an international report that argues that lions, wolves, pumas, lynxes and other major carnivores play key roles in keeping ecosystems in balance. It also warns that the current depletion of numbers of major predators threatens to cause serious ecological problems across the globe.

The paper, written by a group of 14 leading ecologists and biologists from the US, Europe and Australia and published in the journal *Science*, calls for the establishment of an international initiative to conserve large carnivores and help them to coexist with humans. Failure to protect our top predators could soon have devastating consequences, they warn.

"Globally, we are losing our large carnivores," said William Ripple, the report's lead author. "Many of them are endangered and their ranges are collapsing. Many are at risk of extinction, either locally or globally. And, ironically, they are vanishing just as we are learning to appreciate their important ecological effects."

The report has been produced, in part, to show that the classic vision of a large predator, such as a lion or a wolf, being an agent of harm to wildlife and a cause of widespread depletion of animal stocks is misguided. Careful analysis of predators' food chains reveals a very different picture. "In fact, the myriad social and economic effects [of large carnivores] include many benefits," it states.

Ripple, a professor at Oregon State University's department of forest ecosystems and society, and his colleague Robert Beschta, have documented the impact of wolves in Yellowstone and other national parks in North America. When wolf numbers have been reduced, usually by hunters, this has led to an increase in numbers of herbivores, in particular the elk.

Elks browse on trees such as aspen, willow, cottonwood, and various berry-producing shrubs, and the more elks there are, the more browsing damage is done to these trees. The knock-on effect is striking, says the report.

"Local bird populations go down because they have fewer berries to eat," added Ripple. "The same is true of bears, which also eat berries. Beaver populations are also affected. They have less plant life to eat and less wood for making their dams.

"For good measure, the roots of the willow and other shrubs help to hold the soil of river banks together, so they do not get washed away. This does happen, however, when you have no wolves, lots of elks and, therefore, poor levels of vegetation. So you can see that the wolf—which sits at the top of the food chain in midwest America—has an impact that goes right down to having an effect on the shapes of streams."

Yet wolves were once considered to be such a menace that they were exterminated inside Yellowstone national park in 1926. The park's ecology slowly transformed with their absence until, in 1995, they were reintroduced.

"Very quickly, the park's ecosystems returned to normal," said Ripple. "I was impressed with how resilient it proved."

Another example of the ecological importance of large carnivores is provided by lions and leopards. Both animals prey on olive baboons in Africa, and as numbers of these key predators have declined, numbers of olive baboons have increased. The population of lions in particular has been so reduced that it now only covers 17% of its historical range, while numbers of olive baboons have risen in direct proportion.

The consequence of this increase has been significant, say the authors. Olive baboons are omnivores and eat small primates and deer. When olive baboon numbers rise, populations of local monkeys and deer plummet. There is also an effect on human populations.

"Baboons pose the greatest threat to livestock and crops in sub-Saharan Africa, and they use many of the same sources of animal protein and plant foods as humans," states the *Science* paper. "In some areas, baboon raids in agricultural fields require families to keep children out of school so they can help guard planted crops."

Nor is the impact confined to land. Marine carnivores are also being depleted at alarming rates, with similar consequences for ecology of the seabed. Sea otters, which make their homes in the northern Pacific Ocean, control local populations of sea urchins by eating them.

When sea otter populations suffer, urchins do well and this has reverberations along the sea floor. Urchins attack and destroy the giant kelp that is found in vast forests in coastal waters in the Pacific, the scientists point out.

These forests are devastated, often with unfortunate results. Kelp forests dampen currents and storm surges and so protect coasts from erosion and damage. An absence of sea otters means no kelp forest and no seashore protection, in other words.

In addition, kelp absorbs carbon dioxide—just as trees and other plants do on land. And that it is another critical issue, Ripple added.

"Lions, leopards, wolves, sea otters and all those other carnivores at the top of food chains eat herbivores and keep their numbers under control. That in turn means there are fewer animals eating plants and so the planet has more trees or kelp that can absorb carbon dioxide and so help in some way to reduce amounts of the gas in the atmosphere," he said.

The problem for the planet is that across the world very few of the major carnivore populations are stable, the *Science* report reveals. In fact, numbers of virtually all of the major predators—

including tigers, lions, pumas, leopards, cheetahs, jaguars, black bears and hyenas—are plummeting.

More than 75% of the 31 species of large carnivore that were studied are declining, it was found, and 17 species now occupy less than half of their former ranges. According to the report's authors, the majority of the large carnivores that they looked at were either labelled endangered, critically endangered or vulnerable, according to the International Union for the Conservation of Nature.

Unfortunately for the biologists and ecologists who are trying to protect major predators, human tolerance of their presence is low. Farmers find their sheep and cattle are being killed and so view animals such as wolves as a straightforward threat to their livelihoods, for example.

"What is needed is a global initiative that is based on networks of local ecologists, landowners, hunters and other stakeholders who can work together to try to protect our key carnivores," said Ripple.

Carnivores are of immense value, he added. As well as helping protect the environment, they are of considerable tourist appeal. The wolves of Yellowstone bring in millions of dollars of tourist income every year, for example.

"Certainly it is true that these animals are killers, but they are also immensely important to the planet's ecosystems," Ripple told the Observer. "They are hard to live with. But equally they are a precious resource. Yet they are dying out very rapidly. We should not stand by and let that happen."

> *"Although we likely retain a primal fear of predators from the days when our forebears lived among giant ice age carnivores, today we overcompensate for that fear with a penchant for killing that is unknown in the wild."*

Fear of Humans Can Ripple Through Food Webs

Liza Gross

In the following viewpoint, Liza Gross presents research that supports the theory that animals can be afraid of humans to the extent that it affects not only their own habits but carries through an entire food web. Many large prey animals fear humans because of their association with loud voices and guns, which they have learned through close contact with people. The subsequent change in the predators' habits affects all the species below them on the food chain. It can even affect breeding and future generations of species within the food web. Liza Gross is an award-winning independent journalist, investigative reporter and author. Her work has appeared in the Nation, *the* New York Times, *and* Scientific American, *among many others.*

"How Fear of Humans Can Ripple Through Food Webs and Reshape Landscapes," by Liza Gross, The Smithsonian Institution, July 11, 2017. Reprinted by permission.

As you read, consider the following questions:

1. How is human development related to predators' fear of humans?
2. How can fear of humans affect a species' breeding habits?
3. What is meant by a "trophic cascade"? How does the author illustrate this?

O n a rainy night in the Santa Cruz Mountains, a mountain lion feasts on a deer carcass under cover of darkness. The lion dines alone, save for a chorus of tree frogs that start croaking just before he shears off another piece of meat with his powerful jaws. The big cat shakes the water from his head and looks around for a moment, as if searching for the source of the noise, but otherwise seems unfazed by the amphibian choir. Nearly an hour later, the lion is still working on the deer, but the frogs have gone silent.

Suddenly, a man's voice pierces the silence. In a flash, the lion is gone, leaving the remains of his kill. He does not return.

In reality, neither the frogs nor the man were real; both were audio recordings. The big cat, a six-year-old male named 66M, was part of a seven-month "playback" experiment on 17 mountain lions led by Justine Smith, as part of her doctoral research at the University of California at Santa Cruz. Just beyond the deer carcass was a motion-sensitive video cam-speaker system that Smith and her colleagues with the Santa Cruz Puma Project had set up whenever they found fresh kills. The team could usually tell when the mountain lions (also called pumas, cougars and scores of other regional names) had snagged a deer, because their GPS collars revealed that the roving animals had visited the same spot several times during the night.

Upon returning to its kill, a hungry puma triggered a recording of either a human pundit or the familiar, neutral calls of tree frogs, which don't interact with pumas. Nearly all the cats responded like 66M, the team reported in *Proceedings of the Royal Society B* last month. Frogs didn't bother them. But the mere sound of the human voice—in this case, Rush Limbaugh, speaking in an uncharacteristically calm tone—forced the animals to flee and abandon their hard-earned meal. The team concluded that the advent of the human "super predator" may be altering the ecological role of large carnivores—by disrupting the crucial link between a top predator and its prey.

Over the past 10 years, Puma Project research overseen by Chris Wilmers, an associate professor of environmental studies at UC Santa Cruz, has shown that human development affects where the cats move, feed, communicate with each other and stash their kittens. Last year, Smith showed that pumas spend less time feeding near neighborhoods, forcing them to kill more deer. And they're not the only predator slinking away whenever humans are near: African lions, badgers and red foxes are all changing their behavior to avoid humans, with ecological consequences that scientists are just beginning to understand.

"We assumed from the beginning that mountain lions don't like people," Wilmers says. The evidence for that had been correlational, based largely on reading GPS data from radio-collared animals. This latest research, he says, "highly suggests" that the puma's behavioral adaptations are driven by a particular mechanism: fear.

Smith, now a postdoctoral researcher at the University of California at Berkeley, had initially thought pumas living in such a developed landscape would be more habituated to people. "It was very dramatic to see that they fled almost every single time," she says, "and often never returned at all."

Fearsome predators afraid of us? Although we likely retain a primal fear of predators from the days when our forebears lived among giant ice age carnivores, today we overcompensate for that fear with a penchant for killing that is unknown in the wild. At a time when humans have become the dominant influence on the planet—leading many scientists to dub this epoch the Anthropocene, or Age of Humans—it's perhaps not surprising that we distinguish ourselves as killers too.

We kill adult animals, the reproductive future of a species, at up to 14 times the rate seen in wild predators, Chris Darimont and his colleagues reported in a 2015 Science paper. We kill large carnivores at 9 times the rate they kill each other (mostly through intra-species battles). The wide-ranging ecological and evolutionary consequences of our extreme predatory behavior, the scientists argued, "uniquely define humans as a global 'super predator.'" In the Anthropocene, Darimont told me, "humans have turned carnivores into prey."

Only three people have died in mountain lion attacks in California since 1986, according to the California Department of Fish and Wildlife. Pumas, on the other hand, have a long history of dying at the hands of humans. Bounty hunters had largely eradicated the felids east of the Rockies by 1900, and hunted them for decades in California after they became confined to the West. Today, they're typically killed by government officials after picking off someone's pet or livestock. "The highest cause of mortality for pumas in our area is getting shot for eating goats," Smith says. It's no wonder the big cats bolt at the sound of a human voice.

"Understanding fear in the things that should be fearless is one of the coolest and newest [research] areas," says Joel Brown, an evolutionary ecologist at the University of Illinois who was not involved in the puma research. Brown has long studied the larger ecological implications of being afraid, a phenomenon he calls "the ecology of fear."

Scientists used to think mostly about predators' ecological effects in terms of the direct impacts of killing, Brown says. "We now know that fear responses are often more important than the direct killing effect," he says. The mere presence of a predator—signaled by a scent, sudden movement or an approaching shadow—triggers a range of responses in prey species as they try to avoid becoming food. "The mere risk of predation dictates where they forage, when they forage, how much they're willing to forage and how vigilant [they are]," says Brown.

What Happens When Something in a Food Chain Goes Extinct?

A food web, according to the US Geological Survey, is "who eats what." Also called the food chain, the food web describes the series of relationships that occur between predators and prey in an ecosystem. You are a member of the food web if you eat animals that have eaten other animals or plants. Because life forms in a food web depend on one another, the extinction of one species can spell trouble for other life in the ecosystem.

Several types of life forms form the food web. Green plants that can make their own food through photosynthesis are the web's producers. They form the bottom of the chain. Animals that get food from other animals and plants are consumers. Decomposers feed off dead plants and animals because decomposers cannot make their own food. Every member in the food web is a predator, prey or both. For instance, one predator may become the prey for another predator. If one species in the food web ceases to exist, one or more members in the rest of the chain could cease to exist too. A plant or animal doesn't even have to become extinct to affect one of its predators

Theoretical models from the 1970s assumed that risk of predation influenced how animals foraged. This assumption was tested a decade later in pikas, small mountain-dwelling rodents that nest among boulders and also happen to be the inspiration for the Pokemon Pikachu. Nancy Huntly, now an ecologist at Utah State University, created experimental enclosures for the skittish herbivores by carrying boulders out to meadows, far from their dens. Pikas took advantage of these new refugia and promptly moved down the meadow.

In a now classic experiment from 1997, Oswald Schmitz, an ecologist at Yale University, showed that fear can ripple through trophic levels in the food web. Schmitz glued together the mouthparts of grasshopper-eating spiders, to see how grasshoppers

Interrelationships within a food web can be so intricate that a chain of disruptive events can occur when one ecosystem component changes. Polar bears, for example, rely on seals for food. The seal population may decline if Arctic cod, a key food supply for seals, dwindles. Cod eat zooplankton, and zooplankton eat ice algae. If climate change causes sea ice to melt, the ice algae population drops, creating a cascading effect that reduces the polar bear population.

Urbanization and industrialization around a natural habitat may have helped lead to the harelip sucker fish's demise. Humans also affect the food web in other ways. Overfishing occurs when people take too much food from the oceans, and species can't replace themselves. Atlantic cod almost became extinct in the 1900s when fishermen removed too many of those fish from the sea.

While the debate over whether humans affect Earth's temperature continues, weather changes cause negative effects in the food web. As water temperatures rise, the supply of corals decreases. Because other marine life forms live in coral reefs, fewer reefs will lead to disruptions in the food web for creatures that live in the ocean.

"What Happens When Something in a Food Chain Goes Extinct?" Hearst Seattle Media, LLC.

would respond to predators that couldn't kill them. The grasshoppers didn't distinguish between the intact and incapacitated spiders, he found. They changed their feeding behavior when either spider was present, which in turn affected the biomass of the grasses they ate.

Fear can ripple not just through a food web but through future generations. In 2011, Liana Zanette, an expert on predator-induced fear who helped Smith design her puma study, showed that simply hearing the sounds of predators lowers breeding success in songbirds. Zanette used the same type of setup on songbirds in Vancouver's Gulf Islands. Her team removed real predation risk by protecting nests with electric fences to zap hungry raccoons and fishing nets to thwart raptors. Then they manipulated the birds' perception of risk by alternating recordings of raccoons, hawks and other predators—which typically eat half the songbirds' offspring every year—with those of nonthreatening animals like hummingbirds and loons.

"The fear effect was extremely costly for these animals," says Zanette, who is at Western University in Ontario. Females ate less, and so laid fewer eggs. They spent most of their time looking for predators instead of foraging for their nestlings. As a result, these songbird parents produced 40 percent fewer offspring over the breeding season compared to animals that heard nonthreatening sounds.

Last year, Zanette's team used this experimental setup in the same ecosystem to test the idea that fear of large carnivores can ripple through the food web. They focused on raccoons, opportunistic omnivores which their songbird experiments revealed were particularly fond of songbird eggs. It turns out they also love intertidal crabs and fish. With top predators long gone on the Gulf Islands, the fearless coons are free to chow down 24 hours a day, Zanette says.

So she and her student Justin Suraci tried to put the fear of predators back into the gluttonous bandits. They set up speakers and cameras along the shoreline, then played recordings of either dogs (which occasionally kill raccoons) or seals and sea lions (which don't). "When raccoons heard the sounds of barking dogs, they fed 66 percent less than when they heard the sounds of barking seals," Zanette says. "And there was a massive increase in the intertidal fishes and crabs, all the stuff raccoons loved to eat."

If fear produces such dramatic effects through a mesopredator like a raccoon, what might it produce through a top predator like a puma? "We would expect these fear effects to be a common pattern across every single species in the animal world, because being killed by a predator immediately in an attack is such an extremely powerful evolutionary force," says Zanette. Perhaps stating the obvious, she adds: "If you die instantly in a predator attack, your fitness falls to zero."

If people are frightening a top predator to such an extent that it's eating less of its cache, she says, that's clearly going to affect the predator population. But altering the behavior of a large carnivore and how it moves through the landscape will also affect the fear responses of animals in the middle of the food chain and how much they can eat, she says: "And that's going to cause a trophic cascade."

On the positive side, the fact that a top predator fears us enough to avoid us when we're out and about means they can coexist with us, says Smith. But it's a balance. If they become too fearful to traipse through human landscapes, their habitat and hunting grounds will become even more fragmented, drastically reducing their chances of long-term survival.

Smith tries to understand what it's like to live with people from the puma's point of view. "Imagine a zombie apocalypse where there are these dangerous things that they can't comprehend, and they have to hide and slink around like in a zombie movie to find food and navigate the landscape," she says. "We have all these weird sounds and technology, and kill them all the time, but probably in ways they can't predict or perceive. They're kind of living in this postapocalyptic world, trying to escape us."

Periodical and Internet Sources Bibliography

The following articles have been selected to supplement the diverse views presented in this chapter.

Garrick Dutcher, "Do Large Carnivores Keep Their Own Numbers in Check?" Living with Wolves, April 8, 2015. https://www .livingwithwolves.org/2015/04/08/wolf-science-weekly

Darryl Fears, "Decline of Predators Such as Wolves Throws Food Chains Out of Whack, Report Says." *Washington Post*, July 14, 2011. https://www.washingtonpost.com/national/health-science /decline-of-predators-such-as-wolves-throws-food-chains-out -of-whack-report-says/2011/07/14/gIQAaeY1EI_story.html

Christian Gamborg, Clare Palmer, and Peter Sandoe, "Ethics of Wildlife Management and Conservation: What Should We Try to Protect?" Nature Education, 2012. https://www.nature.com /scitable/knowledge/library/ethics-of-wildlife-management-and -conservation-what-80060473

John Hayes, "Top of the Food Chain: Hunters and Other Predators Compete for Game." *Pittsburgh Post-Gazette*, February 19, 2017. https://www.post-gazette.com/life/outdoors/2017/02/19/Hunters -and-other-predators-compete-for-game-in-Pennsylvania -woodlands/stories/201702190102

Jenna Marshall, "Study of Human Impact on Food Webs and Ecosystems Yields Unexpected Insights." Phys.org, February 22, 2019. https://phys.org/news/2019-02-human-impact-food-webs -ecosystems.html

National Geographic, "Food Web." https://www.nationalgeographic .org/encyclopedia/food-web

National Park Service, "Yellowstone National Park: Wolf Restoration." https://www.nps.gov/yell/learn/nature/wolf-restoration.htm

Regional Aquatics Monitoring Program, "Potential Effects from Hunting and Trapping on Aquatic Ecosystems." http://www .ramp-alberta.org/resources/hunting/hunting.aspx

Rosanne Skirble, "Loss of Predators Impacts Food Chain." Voice of America, July 13, 2011. https://www.voanews.com/africa/loss -predators-impacts-food-chain

Joseph Stromberg, "Where Do Humas Really Rank on the Food Chain?" *Smithsonian Magazine*, December 2, 2013. https://www.smithsonianmag.com/science-nature/where-do-humans-really-rank-on-the-food-chain-180948053

Jimmy Tobias, "The Government Agency in Charge of Killing Wild Animals Is Facing Backlash." Pacific Standard, June 24, 2019. https://psmag.com/environment/the-government-agency-in-charge-of-killing-wild-animals-is-finally-facing-backlash

Kimberley Turtenwald, "How Does Hunting Affect the Environment?" Sciencing, April 25, 2018. https://sciencing.com/hunting-affect-environment-11369486.html

Lisa Winter, "5 Reasons to Care About Poaching." A-Plus, July 27, 2016. https://articles.aplus.com/a/5-reasons-to-care-about-poaching?no_monetization=true

Ed Yong, "Shark-Hunting Harms Animals at Bottom of the Food Chain." *National Geographic*, November 8, 2008. https://www.nationalgeographic.com/science/phenomena/2008/11/08/shark-hunting-harms-animals-at-bottom-of-the-food-chain

For Further Discussion

Chapter 1

1. Do you believe it is realistic to claim that hunting and conservation benefit each other? Why? Use information from the viewpoints in this volume to make your case.
2. Do the laws and licensing involved in hunting seem to sufficiently regulate hunting and trapping? If not, what would be a better solution?
3. What other funding sources might be used to pay for conservation efforts, in addition to hunting? Are conservation efforts tainted by money brought in from hunters?

Chapter 2

1. Why are the existing methods for combating illegal trafficking in animals not effective?
2. Using information from this volume, what arguments would you use to explain why a hunting culture is still valuable today?
3. Do you think there is still a definite culture of sport hunting in America today, or is it declining? Provide research to support your answer.

Chapter 3

1. Do you believe there is still a risk of hunting animals to extinction, with so much regulations in place concerning hunting? If so, what is the reason, and how can it be rectified?
2. Is regulated hunting needed to control species overpopulation? Why or why not?
3. What can be said about the relationship between hunting, climate change, and extinction? How are they affecting each other? How does attempting to control one affect the others?

Chapter 4

1. Why is it more difficult now to regulate hunting and how it affects the food chain?
2. How is the role of humans within the food chain shifting? What do you think their role will be in the future?
3. Is it possible to change the relationship between humans and animals as climate change affects the environment?

Organizations to Contact

The editors have compiled the following list of organizations concerned with the issues debated in this book. The descriptions are derived from materials provided by the organizations. All have publications or information available for interested readers. The list was compiled on the date of publication of the present volume; the information provided here may change. Be aware that many organizations take several weeks or longer to respond to inquiries, so allow as much time as possible.

African Wildlife Foundation

1100 New Jersey Ave SE
Suite 900
Washington, DC 20003
(888) 494 5354
email: africanwildlife@awf.org
website: www.awf.org/

The African Wildlife Foundation works to conserve African wildlife and protect the land and habitat that they depend on. They also promote sustainable tourism and agriculture and help develop government policies about wildlife.

Canadian Wildlife Federation

Ottawa–Head Office
350 Michael Cowpland Drive
Kanata, ON K2M 2W1 Canada
(800) 563-9453
email: info@cwf-fcf.org
website: www.cwf-fcf.org/en/

The Canadian Wildlife Federation's mission is to conserve and inspire the conservation of Canada's wildlife and habitats for the use and enjoyment of all. It works with people, corporations, nongovernment organizations, and governments to create collaboration for achieving wildlife conservation.

Ducks Unlimited, Inc.

One Waterfowl Way
Memphis, TN 38120
(800) 45DUCKS
email: via website
website: www.ducks.org/

Ducks Unlimited is an organization dedicated to the conservation of wildfowl and wetlands. It conserves, restores, and managed wetlands and the associated habitats for waterfowl in North America.

National Wildlife Federation

11100 Wildlife Center Drive
Reston, VA 20190
(800) 822-9919
email: via website
website: www.nwf.org/

The National Wildlife Federation is a national organization to increase America's fish and wildlife populations and better help them to thrive in a rapidly changing world by advocating for conservation and wildlife.

The Nature Conservancy

4245 North Fairfax Drive, Suite 100
Arlington, VA 22203-1606
(703) 841-5300
email: member@tnc.org
website: www.nature.org/en-us/

The Nature Conservancy is a global nonprofit organization that works on issues like climate change, food and water sustainability, protecting land and water, and building healthy cities, for both people and animals.

People for the Ethical Treatment of Animals (PETA)

501 Front Street
Norfolk, VA 23510
(757) 622-PETA
email: via website
website: www.peta.org/

PETA is the largest animal rights organization in the world. It is especially focused on areas where animals suffer the most harm, such as animal testing, hunting, the killing of pest animals, and cruelty to domestic animals.

Safari Club International

4800 W. Gates Pass Road
Tucson, AZ 85745
(888) HUNT-SCI
email: via website
website: www.safariclub.org/

Safari Club International is a not-for-profit organization of hunters whose primary missions are to protect the freedom to hunt and to promote wildlife conservation. It has members from all over the world, including chapters in the United States and Canada.

Sierra Club

National Headquarters
2101 Webster Street, Suite 1300
Oakland, CA 94612
(415) 977-5500
email: information@sierraclub.org
website: www.sierraclub.org/

The Sierra Club is one of the oldest environmental organizations in the United States. They work at the grassroots level to fight climate change and protect animals and the environment.

Sportsmen's Alliance

801 Kingsmill Parkway
Columbus, OH 43229
(614) 888-4868
email: info@sportsmensalliance.org
website: www.sportsmensalliance.org/

The Sportsman's Alliance represents hunters and sportsmen, and protects and promotes outdoor heritage of hunting, fishing, trapping and shooting in all fifty state legislatures as well as in the courts, in Congress, and during elections. They also support animal rights.

Wildlife Conservation Society

2300 Southern Boulevard
Bronx, NY 10460
(718) 220-5100
email: via website
website: www.wcs.org/

The Wildlife Conservation Society is a global conservation organization that works in sixty countries to save wildlife and wild places. Their goal is to conserve the world's largest wild places in sixteen priority regions, home to more than 50 percent of the planet's biodiversity.

Bibliography of Books

Nate Blakeslee. *American Wolf: A True Story of Survival and Obsession in the West*. New York, NY: Broadway Books, 2018.

Andrew Butterworth, ed. *Animal Welfare in a Changing World*. Boston, MA: CABI, 2018.

Neil Carr and Donald M. Broom. *Tourism and Animal Welfare*. Boston, MA: CABI, 2018.

Neil Carr and Janette Young, ed. *Wild Animals and Leisure: Rights and Wellbeing* (Routledge Research in the Ethics of Tourism Series*)*. New York, NY: Routledge, 2018.

James Clarke. *Overkill: The Race to Save Africa's Wildlife*. New York, NY: Random House, 2017.

James Clarke. *Save Me from the Lion's Mouth: Exposing Human-Wildlife Conflict in Africa*. New York, NY: Random House, 2013.

David S. Favre. *Respecting Animals: A Balanced Approach to Our Relationship with Pets, Food, and Wildlife*. New York, NY: Prometheus Books, 2018.

Amy J. Fitzgerald. *Animal Advocacy and Environmentalism: Understanding and Bridging the Divide* (Social Movements). New York, NY: Polity Books, 2019.

Gale Research. *Big Game Hunting (Animal Rights and Welfare)*. Farmington Hills, MI: Gale Research, 2018.

Lisa Idzikowski, ed. *Hunting* (Introducing Issues with Opposing Viewpoints). Farmington Hills, MI: Greenhaven, 2019.

Tara Kathleen Kelly. *The Hunter Elite: Manly Sport, Hunting Narratives, and American Conservation, 1880-1925*. Lawrence, KS: University Press of Kansas, 2018.

Nathan Kowalski. *Hunting—Philosophy for Everyone: In Search of the Wild Life*. New York, NY: Wiley-Blackwell, 2010.

Charles J. List. Hunting, *Fishing, and Environmental Virtue: Reconnecting Sportsmanship and Conservation*. Oregon State University Press, 2013.

Richard Louv. *Our Wild Calling: How Connecting with Animals Can Transform Our Lives—and Save Theirs*. New York, NY: Algonquin Books, 2018.

Kevin Markwell, ed. *Animals and Tourism: Understanding Diverse Relationships*. Bristol, UK: Channel View Publications, 2015.

Craig Raleigh. *The Hunter's Way: A Guide to the Heart and Soul of Hunting*. New York, NY: Dey Street Books, 2018.

Steven Rinella. *Meat Eater: Adventures from the Life of an American Hunter*. New York, NY: Spiegel & Grau, 2013.

Peter Singer. *Animal Liberation: The Definitive Classic of the Animal Movement*. New York, NY: Harper Perennial, 2009.

Lamar Underwood, ed. *Theodore Roosevelt on Hunting, Revised and Expanded*. New York, NY: Lyons Press, 2019.

Index

A

ammunition sales, as aiding conservation efforts, 23, 48–53

Angola, 40

antelopes, 46

Antiquities Act, 93

Arizona Game and Fish Department, 42

Audubon Society, 92

B

baboons, 82, 152

Balule nature reserve, 28, 30

bears, 15, 35, 46, 51, 89, 124, 145, 151

bighorn sheep, 36, 42, 45

bison, 22, 46, 92, 99

Boone, Daniel, 92

Boone & Crockett Club, 41, 92

Botswana, 86

Bouba Ndjida National Park, 71

Bove, Jennifer, 120–124

Brutal: Manhood and the Exploitation of Animals, 33

Büchner, Loodt, 83, 84, 85

buffalo, 29, 31

Bukharan markhor, 39, 40

bush babies, 86

bushmeat, 60, 63, 106

C

Cambodia, 73

Cameroon, 71

Canada, 39, 45

cape buffalo, 29, 40

Capps, Ashley, 32–36

Cecil the lion, 83, 84, 88, 89–90, 91, 93, 102, 103

chameleons, 86

Cheney, Dick, 46

Chinese medicine, 64, 75

Conservation Force, 40

consumptive management, explanation of, 23

Convention on International Trade in Endangered Species of Wild Fauna and Flora (CITES), 60, 63, 66, 76

cougars, 15, 46, 51

Coutada 11 hunting area, 40

crime syndicates, involvement in wildlife smuggling/poaching, 60, 62, 64, 65, 73

Crockett, Davy, 92

D

Dasgupta, Shreya, 137–143

deer farms, 32, 34

deer population, using hunting to manage, 15, 41, 107–113

DNA tracking, 65

dogs, 46

Duck Stamp, 23
Ducks Unlimited, 39

E

eagles, 86, 124
eco tourism, 77
elephants, 15, 18, 24, 25, 26, 30, 36, 45, 57, 60, 62, 63–64, 70, 71, 72, 80, 81, 82, 86, 93, 94, 102–103, 123, 143
elk, 51, 151
Endangered Species Act, 99
environmental crime, explanation of, 70
Ethiopia, 25
excise taxes, on firearms and ammunition, 23, 48–53
Executive Order 13648 on Combating Wildlife Trafficking, 61

F

fear effect, explanation of, 114–119
Federal Aid in Sport Fish Restoration Act (Dingell-Johnson Act), 59
Federal Aid in Wildlife Restoration Act (Pittman-Robertson Act), 23, 48–53
Federal Migratory Bird Hunting and Conservation Stamp, 23
firearm accidents, 15, 46
firearm sales, as aiding conservation efforts, 23, 48–53
Fitzpatrick, Brad, 37–42

Foundation for North American Wild Sheep, 42
foxes, 44, 46

G

game breeding, 22
giraffes, 29, 82
gorillas, 106, 124
GPS chipping, 65
Grand Canyon, 93
Grant, Ulysses S., 92
great auk, 44, 99
Gross, Liza, 154–161
grouse, 51
Gurafarda rainforests, 25

H

Hearst Seattle Media, 158–159
heath hen, 99
hippopotamus, 29
Høgh, Jens Ulrik, 82, 83, 84
hornbills, 86
Hunt, Elle, 80–87
hunting
   as aiding conservation, 18–19, 20–26, 27–31, 32–36, 37–42, 43–47, 48–53
   as fostering negative attitude toward animals, 57–58, 59–68, 69–79, 80–87, 88–95
   impact on food chain, 136, 137–143, 144–148, 149–153, 154–161

and increase in extinction, 18,
98–99, 101–106, 107–113,
114–119, 120–124, 125–132

hunting license fees, and
conservation funding, 18

Hwange National Park, 91

hyenas, 30

I

International Consortium on
Combating Wildlife Crime
(ICCWC), 76

International Council for Game
and Wildlife Conservation, 40

International Criminal Police
Organization (INTERPOL), 76,
143

International Union for
Conservation of Nature
(IUCN), 40, 65, 121

ivory, 60, 62, 63–64, 70–72,
102–103

Izaak Walton League, 47

K

Karner blue butterfly, 51

Kenya, 24

Khan, Shehab, 75

Klaserie nature reserve, 28, 30

Kruger National Park, 28, 90

L

Lao People's Democratic Republic,
73

lemurs, 105–106

Limpopo Travel & Diana Hunting
Tours, 82

Lin, Doris, 35

lions, 18, 24, 26, 30 57, 80, 82, 83,
84, 85, 86, 88, 89, 90–91, 93,
102, 103, 149–153

Luke, Brian, 33

Lyme disease, 15

M

Malaysia, 76

McKie, Robin, 149–153

meat hunting, compared to trophy
hunting, 24–25

Migratory Bird Conservation
Fund, 50

migratory bird species,
conservation efforts to preserve,
22, 23

Miller, Jennie, 114–119

Mills, John, 144–148

Milman, Oliver, 88–95

Monitoring the Illegal Killing of
Elephants (MIKE), 63

Mozambique, 40

Myanmar, 73, 74

N

Namibia, 24, 30, 85, 94

National Audubon Society, 46

national parks, and species
protection, 23–24, 25, 92

National Parks and Conservation
Association, 47

National Wildlife Federation, 46

National Wildlife Refuge System, 22, 23

National Wild Turkey Federation, 41

nature reserves, compared to tourist lodges, 28–31

Nile crocodiles, 26

non-consumptive management, explanation of, 23

non-native species, and conservation, 125–132

North American Model of Wildlife Conservation, 22, 49

O

Olden, Julian D., 125–132

P

Palmer, Walter, 83, 89–90, 91

Panthera, 40

partridges, 34

passenger pigeon, 22, 99, 116

People for the Ethical Treatment of Animals (PETA), 43–47

pheasants, 34, 35

Phelan, Jessica, 101–106

photographic tourism, 25, 29

poachers, 21, 40, 44, 45, 47, 57, 59–68, 69–79, 86, 101–106, 121–123, 137, 138, 143, 149

Pursell, Allen, 107–113

Q

quail, 34

R

rhinoceros, 60, 62, 63, 64–66, 70, 71, 72, 73, 75, 77, 94, 103–104, 123, 138, 143

Rocky Mountain Elk Foundation, 39

Roosevelt, Theodore, 14, 22, 41, 49, 57, 88, 89, 92–94

Roussos, Jason, 20–26

S

safaris, 20, 22, 27, 28, 57, 83, 94, 102

Sales, Graham, 90

Santa Catalina Mountains, 42

Satao the elephant, 103

Sax, Dov F., 125–132

Schipani, Sam, 48–53

Schlaepfer, Martin A., 125–132

Scientific Arguments Against Hunting, 35

SCI Foundation, 39

Scott, Don, 28, 29, 31

sea turtles, 105

Segage, Martina, 31

Sheikh, Pervaze A., 59–68

Sierra Club, 46

snakes, 86

South Africa, 30, 72, 81, 85, 90, 94

sturgeon caviar, 60

Switlyk, Larysa, 81, 82

T

Tajikistan, 39, 40

Tanda Tula, 28

Tanzania, 24, 30, 85

Tasmanian tiger, 44

Thomson, Ron, 81, 86

ticks, 15

tigers, 15, 70, 71, 72, 73, 75, 77, 104

Timbavati nature reserve, 28, 29, 31

timber, illicit logging of, 70, 73–74, 76, 77

Tootabi Hunting Safaris, 83, 84

tourist lodges, compared to nature reserves, 28–31

trophy hunters, profiles of, 80–87

trophy hunting, how it helps conservation, 18, 20–26, 27–31

turkeys, 23, 41, 46, 50, 51, 62, 89

Turner, Ted, 45

U

Umbabat nature reserve, 28, 30

United Nations, 69–79

United Nations Office on Drugs and Crime (UNODC), 76, 77, 78

United States Environmental Protection Agency, 116–117

United States Fish and Wildlife Service, 16, 23 95

V

Virunga National Park, 106

W

waterfowl preservation, 39

Weldy, Troy, 107–113

What Will Happen to Animals If Everyone Goes Vegan?, 35

White, Mark, 107–113

white-tailed deer, 15, 35, 36, 41, 50, 108–113

Whitworth, Jared, 90

Wilderness Society, 47

Wildlife and Forest Crime Analytic Toolkit, 76

wildlife smuggling/black market, 38, 59–68, 69–79

Wilson-Spath, Andreas, 27–31

Wisconsin, 32, 34–35, 111

Wisconsin Department of Agriculture, Trade and Consumer Protection, 24–35

wolves, 15, 44, 124, 149–153

World Customs Organization, 76

World Wildlife Fund (WWF), 47, 75, 77

Wyler, Liana Sun, 59–68

X

Xanda the lion, 90–91

Y

Yellowstone, 92, 151, 153

Z

zebras, 82

Zimbabwe, 30, 40, 81, 83, 85, 90, 91, 102, 105

zoos, 22